D0909615

QUESTIONS
YOUNG
PEOPLE
ASK
ANSWERS THAT WORK

QUESTIONS
YOUNG PEOPLE ASK
ANSWERS THAT WORK

© 1989
WATCH TOWER BIBLE AND TRACT SOCIETY OF PENNSYLVANIA
All rights reserved

Publishers
WATCHTOWER BIBLE AND TRACT SOCIETY OF NEW YORK, INC.
INTERNATIONAL BIBLE STUDENTS ASSOCIATION
Brooklyn, New York, U.S.A.

This Book Is Published in 46 Languages
Total Books Printed of All Editions:
19,100,000 Copies

Unless otherwise indicated,
Scripture quotations are from the modern-language
New World Translation of the Holy Scriptures—With References, 1984 Edition

Picture Credits
Pictures are listed by page number and by order of appearance on page, top to bottom.
Bronx Zoo; photographed and used with the kind cooperation of: page 195 (2)
National Aeronautics and Space Administration, Washington, D.C.:
pages 307, 311 (background)
National Archives, Washington, D.C.: page 304 (background)

Questions Young People Ask
Answers That Work
English (*yp*-E)
Made in the United States of America

Answers That Work

'WHY DON'T my parents understand me?' 'Should I give drugs and alcohol a try?' 'What about sex before marriage?' 'How do I know if it's real love?' 'What does the future hold for me?'

You are neither the first—nor the last—youth to ask such questions. However, when young people raise these basic issues, they are often barraged with conflicting answers. For example, drinking alcoholic beverages. Parents may discourage it—though indulging in it themselves. Magazines and TV shows glorify it. Peers encourage you to try it. No wonder, then, that many youths are genuinely perplexed as to just what they should do.

Recognizing the need for honest, workable answers to the questions of today's youth, *Awake!* magazine* inaugurated a feature entitled "Young People Ask . . ." in January 1982. The series immediately drew a favorable reader response. "The series is evidence of your continued interest in the plight of young people today," wrote one appreciative reader. "I hope and pray that these articles never end," wrote another.

Yet another young reader put it this way: 'I am 14 years old and I never knew growing up could be so hard. There is so much pressure on young kids today. That is why I am very grateful for the articles. Every night I thank God for having them published.' The articles, however, were not childish, nor was any attempt made to "write down" to our readers. "Young People Ask . . ." thus found an appreciative audience among adults. "I am

---

* Published semimonthly by the Watchtower Bible and Tract Society of New York, Inc.

40 years of age," wrote one parent. "These articles are truly godsends to us parents." Christian elders found them particularly useful in understanding young ones in congregations of Jehovah's Witnesses and in dealing with them.

Why has "Young People Ask . . . " triggered such enthusiastic response? The answers given really *work!* Each article is the product of extensive research. Furthermore, in order to determine just how young people really think and feel, *Awake!* reporters have spoken to hundreds of young people all over the world! Their candid expressions have been of great help in making the articles realistic and practical.

However, the real secret to the success of "Young People Ask . . . " lies in the fact that the answers given have been based, not upon theory or personal opinion, but upon the eternal truths found in God's Word, the Bible. *'The Bible?'* you may ask. Yes, it has much to say to young people. (See Proverbs, chapters 1-7; Ephesians 6:1-3.) It was inspired by our Creator, who is keenly aware of "the desires incidental to youth." (2 Timothy 2:20-22; 3:16) And while human society has changed much since Bible times, youthful desires have changed little. The Bible is thus as current as ever. We have endeavored, though, to present the Bible's counsel in such a way that youths do not feel preached to, but, rather, reasoned with. And while the material has been written primarily with youths among Jehovah's Witnesses in mind, it can be read and enjoyed by anyone who has respect for the practical wisdom contained in the Bible.

In response to the requests of many readers, we have compiled a number of "Young People Ask . . . " articles in book form. The 39 chapters herein represent, in condensed form, information from over 100 of the nearly 200 articles that appeared in *Awake!* between 1982 and 1989. Some fresh material has been added. Furthermore, it is richly illustrated with photographs of youths of different lands and races.

Feel free to scan the table of contents and go right to the questions that concern you the most. We recommend, though, that you later take the time to read the book through in its entirety, looking up the scriptures in your own copy of the Bible.

In some families, parent-child communication is lacking or awkward at best. We have thus added a feature called Questions for Discussion, which appears at the end of each chapter. The questions are not designed for paragraph-by-paragraph analysis. Nor are they a vehicle for parents to quiz their children. They are designed to stimulate discussions between youths and parents. Many of the questions allow you to give your own point of view or to apply the material under discussion to your own situation.

Many families may therefore want to use this book at times as a basis for family study. Family members might do so by taking turns reading paragraphs, looking up any scriptures cited. The Questions for Discussion can be asked intermittently, as appropriate subheadings are completed or after the whole chapter has been completed. All can be encouraged to express their feelings openly and honestly. Young people may enjoy discussing the book among themselves.

These are "critical times hard to deal with," even for young people. (2 Timothy 3:1) With a knowledge of God's Word, however, you can successfully pass through that difficult time of life. (Psalm 119:9) It is our pleasure, therefore, to provide this collection of practical, Bible-based answers to questions that may perplex you.

_____*The Publishers*

Contents

Section 1   The Home Front: Dealing With Family Members

Chapter	Page	
1	11	Why Should I 'Honor My Father and My Mother'?
2	18	Why Don't My Parents Understand Me?
3	26	How Can I Get My Folks to Give Me More Freedom?
4	34	Why Did Dad and Mom Split Up?
5	42	How Can I Deal With My Parent's Remarriage?
6	50	Why Are My Brother and Sister So Hard to Get Along With?
7	56	Should I Leave Home?

Section 2   You and Your Peers

Chapter	Page	
8	65	How Can I Make Real Friends?
9	73	How Can I Cope With Peer Pressure?

Section 3   A Look at How You Look

Chapter	Page	
10	82	How Important Are Looks?
11	90	Do My Clothes Reveal the Real Me?

Section 4   Why Do I Feel This Way?

Chapter	Page	
12	98	Why Don't I Like Myself?
13	104	Why Do I Get So Depre...
14	115	How Can I Ma...
15	121	Why A...
16	12...	

Section 6   Sex and Morals

Chapter	Page	
21	166	How Can I Get (and Keep) a Job?
22	174	What Career Should I Choose?
23	181	What About Sex Before Marriage?
24	192	How Can I Say No to Premarital Sex?
25	198	Masturbation—How Serious Is It?
26	205	Masturbation—How Can I Fight the Urge?
27	212	Honesty—Is It Really the Best Policy?

Section 7   Dating, Love, and the Opposite Sex

Chapter	Page	
28	219	How Can I Get Over a Crush?
29	225	Am I Ready to Date?
30	236	Am I Ready for Marriage?
31	242	How Do I Know If It's Real Love?
32	252	How Can I Carry On a Successful Courtship?

Section 8   The Trap of Drugs and Alcohol

Chapter	Page	
33	262	Drinki...
34	3...	

Chapter 1

Why Should I 'Honor My Father and My Mother'?

"HONOR your father and your mother." To many youths these words sound like something out of the Dark Ages.

Young Veda declared open rebellion against her father by dating a boy who abused drugs and alcohol. Defiantly, she would also go out dancing till the early morning hours. "I felt that he was too strict," Veda explains. "I was 18 years old, and I thought I knew it all. I felt my father was mean and just didn't want me to have a good time, so I went out and did what I wanted to do."

Most youths would probably disapprove of Veda's actions. Yet, if their parents ordered them to clean their room, do their homework, or be in by a certain hour, many would seethe with resentment or, worse yet, would openly defy their parents! How a youth views his parents, though, can ultimately mean not only the difference between war and peace at home but also his very life. For the command to 'honor your parents' comes from God, and he attaches the following incentive to heeding this commandment: "That it may go well with you and you may endure a long time on the earth." (Ephesians 6:2, 3) The stakes are high. Let us, therefore, take a fresh look at what honoring your father and your mother really means.

What 'Honoring' Them Means

"Honor" involves recognizing duly constituted authority. For instance, Christians are commanded to

How should you view your parents' rules?

"have honor for the king." (1 Peter 2:17) While you may not always agree with a national ruler, his position or office is still to be respected. Similarly, God has vested parents with certain authority in the family. This means that you must recognize their God-given right to make rules for you. True, other parents may be more lenient than yours are. Your parents, though, have the job of deciding what is best for *you*—and different families may have different standards.

It is also true that even the best of parents can occasionally be arbitrary—even unfair. But at Proverbs 7:1, 2 one wise parent said: "My son [or daughter], . . . keep my commandments and continue living." Likewise, your parents' rules, or "commandments," are usually intended for your good and are an expression of their genuine love and concern.

John, for example, had repeatedly been told by his

mother that he should always use the walkway over the six-lane highway near their home. One day, two girls from school dared him to take the shortcut across the road itself. Ignoring their taunts of "chicken!" John took the walkway. Partway across, John heard the sound of screeching tires. Looking down, he watched in horror as the two girls were hit by a car and hurled into the air! Granted, obeying your parents is seldom a matter of life and death. Nevertheless, obedience usually benefits you.

'Honoring your parents' also means accepting correction, not sulking or throwing tantrums when it is administered. Only a fool "disrespects the discipline of his father," says Proverbs 15:5.

Finally, showing honor means more than just rendering formal respect or begrudging obedience. The original Greek verb rendered "honor" in the Bible basically means to consider someone as of great value. Parents should thus be viewed as precious, highly esteemed, and dear to you. This involves having warm, appreciative feelings for them. However, some youths have anything *but* warm feelings toward their parents.

Problem Parents—Worthy of Honor?

A youth named Gina wrote: "My dad drank so much, and I couldn't sleep because my parents would argue and shout a lot. I would lie on the bed and just cry. I could not tell them how I felt about it because my mom would probably hit me. The Bible says 'honor thy father,' but I can't."

Parents who are hot-tempered or immoral, who are drunkards, or who bicker with each other—are they really worthy of honor? Yes, for the Bible condemns holding any parent "in derision." (Proverbs 30:17)

Proverbs 23:22 further reminds us that your parents have "caused your birth." This alone is reason to honor them. Gregory, who at one time was very disrespectful, now says: "I thank Jehovah God that [my mother] didn't abort me or dump me in a garbage can as a baby. She is a single parent, and there were six of us. I know it was tough on her."

Though they are less than perfect, your parents have also made many sacrifices for you. "One time all we had left to eat was a can of corn and some grits," continues Gregory. "My mom fixed it for us kids, but she didn't eat. I went to bed full, but I kept wondering why Mom didn't eat. Now that I have my own family, I

Must you honor parents whose conduct is reproachful?

14   YOUNG PEOPLE ASK . . .

realize she was sacrificing for us." (One research study puts the cost of raising a child to age 18 at $66,400.)

Realize, too, that just because a parent's example is not the best, this does not mean that everything he or she tells you is wrong. In Jesus' day, the religious leaders were corrupt. Yet, Jesus told the people: "All the things they tell you, do and observe, but do not do according to their deeds." (Matthew 23:1-3, 25, 26) Could not this principle be applied to some parents?

Dealing With Feelings of Resentment

What if you feel that a parent is seriously abusing his or her authority?* Stay calm. Rebelling accomplishes nothing, neither does hateful, spiteful behavior. (Ecclesiastes 8:3, 4; compare Ecclesiastes 10:4.) One 17-year-old girl came to resent her parents because they were preoccupied with their own squabbles and seemed indifferent toward her. Resentment toward them was then directed toward the Bible principles her parents had tried to teach her. Out of sheer spite, she ventured into sexual immorality and drug abuse. "I felt I owed my parents one," was her bitter explanation. But by being spiteful, she only hurt herself.

The Bible warns: "Take care that rage does not allure you into spiteful [actions] . . . Be on your guard that you do not turn to what is hurtful." (Job 36:18-21) Realize that parents are responsible before Jehovah for their conduct and will answer for any serious injustices. —Colossians 3:25.

Proverbs 19:11 says: "The insight of a man certainly slows down his anger, and it is beauty on his part to pass over transgression." At times it is best to try to

---

* We are not referring here to cases of physical or sexual abuse in which a youth may need to seek professional help from outside the home.

forgive and forget a parent's hurtful actions. Rather than dwell on his faults, focus on his good qualities. Dody, for example, had an insensitive mom and an alcoholic stepdad. Notice how her insight into their shortcomings stifled bitterness. She says: "Perhaps my mom never showed us love because, as an abused child, she was never taught how. My stepfather showed an interest in our activities when he was sober, but that wasn't very often. Yet, my sister and I always had a roof over our heads and food in the refrigerator."

> "*I* felt my father was mean and just didn't want me to have a good time, so I went out and did what I wanted to do"

Fortunately, wayward or neglectful parents are a minority. More than likely your parents take an interest in you and try to set a good example. Even so, you may feel some resentment toward them at times. "Sometimes when I was discussing a problem with Mom and she couldn't see my point," admits a young man named Roger, "I'd get mad and say something out of spite just to hurt her. It was my way of getting back at her. But when I walked away, I felt so bad, and I knew she didn't feel good either."

Thoughtless words may 'stab' and 'cause pain,' but they will not solve your problems. "The tongue of the wise ones is a healing." (Proverbs 12:18; 15:1) "Though it was hard, I would go back and apologize," explains Roger. "I could then discuss the problem more calmly, and we could get it solved."

'What My Dad Said Was Right'

Interestingly, some youths wear themselves and their parents out resisting parental instructions, only to

YOUNG PEOPLE ASK . . .

find out later that their parents were right all along. Consider Veda (mentioned at the outset), for example. She went out riding with her boyfriend one day. He was high on marijuana and beer. The car went out of control and struck a lamppost at 60 miles per hour. Veda survived—with a deep gash on her forehead. The boyfriend fled the scene, never even showing up at the hospital to help her.

"When my parents arrived at the hospital," confessed Veda, "I told them that everything my dad had said was right and that I should have listened a long time ago. . . . I had made a big mistake, and it almost cost my life." After that, Veda made some big changes in her attitude toward her parents.

Perhaps some changes would be appropriate on your part too. 'Honoring your parents' may indeed seem to be an old-fashioned idea. But not only is it the smart thing to do it is also the *right* thing to do in the eyes of God. What, though, if you want to show your parents respect but feel misunderstood or perhaps hemmed in by restrictions? Let's examine how you can improve your lot in such situations.

Questions for Discussion   Chapter 1

☐ *What does it mean to honor one's parents?*

☐ *Why do parents make so many rules? Can those rules benefit you?*

☐ *Do you have to honor your parents if their conduct is reproachful? Why?*

☐ *What are some productive ways of dealing with the resentment you might occasionally feel toward your parents? What are some foolish ways?*

Chapter 2

Why Don't My Parents Understand Me?

IT'S only human to want to be understood. And if your parents are critical of—or uninterested in—things you love or think are important, you can feel very frustrated.

Sixteen-year-old Robert feels that his father does not understand his choice of music. "All he does is scream and say, 'Turn it off!'" said Robert. "So I turn *it* and *him* off." Many youths similarly withdraw emotionally into their own private world when parental understanding seems to be lacking. In one extensive study of youths, 26 percent of the youths surveyed admitted, "I try to stay away from home most of the time."

A huge rift, or gap, between youths and parents thus exists in many homes. What causes it?

"Power" Versus "Gray-Headedness"

Proverbs 20:29 states: "The beauty of young men [or women] is their power." This strength, or "power," though, can lay the groundwork for all sorts of conflicts between you and your parents. The proverb continues: "And the splendor of old men is their gray-headedness." Your parents may not literally be 'gray-headed,' but they are older and tend to view life differently. They realize that not every situation in life has a happy ending. Bitter personal experience may have tempered the idealism they once had as youths. Because of this wisdom born of experience—"gray-headedness," as it were—they just may not share your enthusiasm over certain matters.

Says young Jim: "My parents (depression-era children) feel that money should be saved to buy or spend on things of importance. But I am living right now too. . . . I want to travel a lot." Yes, between one's youthful "power" and one's parents' "gray-headedness" may lie a huge gap. Many families are thus bitterly divided over issues such as dress and grooming, behavior with the opposite sex, use of drugs and alcohol, curfews, associates, and chores. The generation gap can be bridged. But before you can expect your parents to understand you, you must try to understand them.

Parents Are Human Too

"When I was younger, I naturally felt that Mom was 'perfect' and didn't have any of the weaknesses and feelings I had," says John. Then his parents divorced, leaving his mother to care for seven children alone. John's sister April recalls: "I remember seeing her cry because of the frustration of trying to keep up with everything. Then I realized we had a wrong viewpoint. She can't do everything always at the right time and in the right way. We saw that she had feelings and was human too."

Recognizing that your parents are simply humans with feelings like yours is a big step toward your

How Can I Tell My Parents?

The task of confessing a wrong to your folks is not pleasant. Young Vince says: "I always sensed that my parents had a lot of trust in me and that made it difficult for me to approach them because I didn't want to hurt them."

Youths who resort to cover-ups often suffer the pangs of a wounded conscience. (Romans 2:15) Their errors can become "a heavy load," too weighty to bear. (Psalm 38:4) Almost inevitably, they are forced to deceive their parents by lying, thereby committing further wrongs. Their relationship with God is thus damaged.

The Bible says: "He that is covering over his transgressions will not succeed, but he that is confessing and leaving them will be shown mercy." (Proverbs 28:13) As 19-year-old Betty puts it: "Jehovah sees everything anyway."

If the matter involves serious wrongdoing, seek Jehovah's forgiveness, confessing your wrong in prayer. (Psalm 62:8) Next, tell your parents. (Prov-

erbs 23:26) They have experience in life and can often help you leave your mistakes behind and avoid repeating them. "It really can help you to talk about it," reports 18-year-old Chris. "It's finally a relief to get it off your mind." The problem is, _how_ do you tell your parents?

The Bible speaks of "a word spoken at the right time for it." (Proverbs 25:11; compare Ecclesiastes 3:1, 7.) When might that be? Chris continues: "I wait until suppertime and then tell Dad that I need to talk to him." The son of a single parent tried yet another time: "I would usually talk to Mom right before bedtime; she'd be more relaxed then. When she came home from work, she was all wound up."

Perhaps you might say something like, "Mom and Dad, something is troubling me." And what if your parents seem too busy to care? You might say, "I know you're busy, but something is really troubling me. Can we talk?" You might then ask: "Did you ever do

Choose a time when your parents might be in a more receptive frame of mind

something that you were too ashamed to talk about?"

Now comes the hard part: telling your parents about the wrong itself. Be humble and "speak truth," not watering down the seriousness of your error or trying to withhold some of the more unpleasant details. (Ephesians 4:25; compare Luke 15:21.) Use words your folks will understand, not expressions that carry a special meaning only to young people.

Naturally, your parents may feel hurt and disappointed at first. So don't be surprised or indignant if you are hit with an emotion-packed volley of words! If you had heeded their earlier warnings, you probably wouldn't be in this situation. So stay calm. (Proverbs 17: 27) Listen to your folks and answer their questions, regardless of how they ask them.

No doubt your earnestness about setting matters straight will make a deep impression on them. (Compare 2 Corinthians 7:11.) Nevertheless, be prepared to accept some well-deserved discipline. "True, no discipline seems for the present to be joyous, but grievous; yet afterward to those who have been trained by it it yields peaceable fruit, namely, righteousness." (Hebrews 12:11) Remember, too, that this will not be the last time you will need your parents' help and mature advice. Get into the habit of confiding in them about small problems so that when the big problems come along, you won't fear telling them what's on your mind.

understanding them. They might, for example, feel very insecure about their ability to rear you properly. Or, feeling overwhelmed by all the moral dangers and temptations you face, they may tend to overreact to things at times. They also may be contending with physical, financial, or emotional hardships. A father, for instance, may hate his job but may never complain. So when his child says, "I can't stand school," it is no wonder that rather than respond sympathetically, he retorts, "What's the matter with you? You kids have it easy!"

Take a "Personal Interest"

How, then, can you find out how your parents feel? By "keeping an eye, not in personal interest upon just your own matters, but also in personal interest upon those of the others." (Philippians 2:4) Try asking your mother what she was like as a teenager. What were her feelings, her goals? "Chances are," said *'Teen* magazine, "that if she feels that you're interested in, and aware of the reasons for some of *her* feelings, she'll try to be more aware of *yours*." The same would no doubt be true of your father.

> *"If [your mother] feels that you're interested in, and aware of the reasons for some of her feelings, she'll try to be more aware of yours."*—'Teen *magazine*

If a conflict arises, do not be quick to accuse your folks of being insensitive. Ask yourself: 'Was my parent not feeling well or worried about something? Was he or she perhaps hurt over some thoughtless deed or word on my part? Do they simply misunderstand what I mean?' (Proverbs 12:18) Showing such empathy is a good start at closing that generation gap. Now you can

You may likewise find that speaking 'straight from the heart' can help settle many misunderstandings.

Handling Disagreements

This does not mean, however, that your parents will immediately come to view things your way. You must therefore keep a grip on your emotions. "All his spirit [impulses] is what a stupid one lets out, but he that is wise keeps it calm to the last." (Proverbs 29:11) *Calmly* discuss the merits of your viewpoint. Stick to the issues instead of arguing that "everybody else does it!"

At times your parents are going to say no. This does not mean they do not understand you. They may simply want to forestall disaster. "My mother is strict on me," admits one 16-year-old girl. "It bothers me that she tells me I can't do something, or [that I must] come into the house at a certain time. But deep down inside, she really cares. . . . she looks out for me."

The security and warmth that mutual understanding brings to a family is beyond words. It makes the home a haven in times of anguish. But real effort is needed on the part of everyone involved.

Questions for Discussion   *Chapter 2*

☐ *Why do youths and parents often conflict?*

☐ *How might a better understanding of your parents affect your view of them?*

☐ *How can you come to understand your parents better?*

☐ *Why does leading a double life deepen the rift between you and your parents?*

☐ *Why is it best to let parents know when you are having serious problems? How can you go about telling them?*

☐ *How can you help your parents understand you better?*

Chapter 3

How Can I Get My Folks to Give Me More Freedom?

YOU say you're old enough to stay out late on weekends. *They* say you have to be home early. *You* say you want to see that new movie everybody is talking about. *They* say you can't see it. *You* say you've met some nice kids you'd like to go out with. *They* say they'd like to meet your friends first.

When you're a teenager, it can sometimes feel as if your parents have a choke hold on your life. It seems that every "I want to" you say is followed by an inevitable "No, you can't." Nor is any part of your life safe from the "prying eyes" of your parents. Says 15-year-old Debbie: "My dad always wants to know where I am, what time I'm going to be home. Most parents do that. Do they have to know *everything?* They should give me more freedom."

Youths further complain that their parents do not respect them. Instead of being trusted, they are judged guilty without a trial when something goes wrong. Instead of being allowed to choose for themselves, they are hemmed in by rules.

"Mental Distress"

Do your folks sometimes treat you like a small child? If so, remember that not too long ago you really *were* a child. Your parents' image of you as a helpless infant is

YOUNG PEOPLE ASK . . .

quite fresh in their minds and not so easily set aside. They still remember the childish mistakes you used to make and thus want to protect you—whether you want such protection or not.

That urge to protect you is a powerfully strong one. When Mom and Dad aren't busy putting a roof over your head, clothing you, or feeding you, they are often grappling with the problems of how to teach, train, and, yes, protect you. Their interest in you is far from casual. They are responsible before God for the way in which they bring you up. (Ephesians 6:4) And when something seems to threaten your well-being, they worry.

Consider Jesus Christ's parents. After a visit to Jerusalem, they unknowingly left for home without him. When they became aware of his absence, they made a diligent—even frantic—search for him! And when they finally "found him in the temple," Jesus' mother exclaimed,

Do you feel that your parents fence you in?

"Child, why did you treat us this way? Here your father and I *in mental distress* have been looking for you." (Luke 2:41-48) Now if Jesus—a perfect child—caused his parents anxiety, think of how much worry you must cause your parents!

Take, for example, that never-ending conflict over what time you should come home. Perhaps you see no reason to be restricted in this way. But have you ever looked at matters from your parents' point of view? The school-age authors of the book *The Kids' Book About Parents* tried to do so. They compiled a list of what they called "the fantasies that must go on in parents' heads about what their kids are doing if they are not home at the proper time." Included in this list were such things as 'doing drugs, getting in a car accident, hanging out in parks, getting arrested, going to porno movies, selling dope, getting raped or mugged, winding up in jail, and disgracing the family name.'

Not all parents would jump to such seemingly far-fetched conclusions. But is it not true that many young people *are* involved in such things? So should you resent the suggestion that keeping both late hours and the wrong kind of company could be harmful? Why even Jesus' parents wanted to know his whereabouts!

Why They Smother

Some youths say that their parents' fear of harm coming to them borders on paranoia! But remember, much time and emotion have been invested in you. The thought of your growing up and eventually leaving may disturb your parents. Wrote one parent: "My only child, a son, is nineteen now, and I can hardly bear the idea of his moving out."

Some parents thus tend to smother or to overprotect their children. It would be a real mistake, though,

YOUNG PEOPLE ASK . . .

for you to overreact in turn. One young woman recalls: "Until I reached the age of about 18, my mother and I were *very* close. . . . [But] as I got older we started to have problems. I wanted to exert some independence, which she must have seen as a threat to our relationship. She, in turn, started to try to hold on to me tighter, and I reacted by pulling away more."

A measure of independence is fine, but don't obtain it at the cost of your family ties. How can you set your relationship with your parents on a more adult footing, based on mutual understanding, tolerance, and respect? For one thing, respect begets respect. The apostle Paul once recalled: "We used to have fathers who were of our flesh to discipline us, and *we used to give them respect.*" (Hebrews 12:9) The parents of these early Christians were not infallible. Paul continued (verse 10): "Our human fathers . . . could only do what they thought best."—*The Jerusalem Bible.*

> *"My dad always wants to know where I am, what time I'm going to be home. . . . Do they have to know everything?"*

At times these men erred in their judgment. Yet they merited their children's respect. So do your parents. The fact that they may be the smothering type is no reason to be rebellious. Give them the same respect you want for yourself.

Misunderstandings

Have you ever been late getting home because of circumstances beyond your control? Did your parents overreact? Such misunderstandings provide another opportunity for you to win respect. Recall how young Jesus handled himself when his upset parents finally

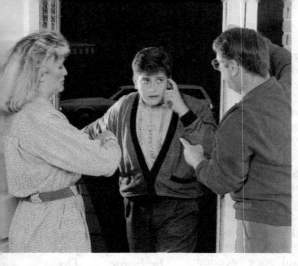

*R*emaining calm when misunderstandings have occurred is one way to gain respect

found him in the temple, innocently discussing God's Word with some teachers. Did Jesus launch into an emotional tirade, cry, or whine about how unfair it was of them to impugn his motives? Note his calm reply: "Why did you have to go looking for me? Did you not know that I must be in the house of my Father?" (Luke 2:49) No doubt Jesus' parents were impressed by the maturity he here displayed. "An answer, when mild," thus not only "turns away rage" but can also help win your parents' respect.—Proverbs 15:1.

Rules and Regulations

How you respond to your parents' demands also has a lot to do with how you will be treated. Some youths sulk, lie, or openly disobey. Try a more adult approach. If you want permission to stay out late, don't make childish demands or whine that "all the other kids can stay out late." Writer Andrea Eagan advises: "[Tell] them as much as you can about what it is you want to do, so that they really understand the situation. . . . If you tell them all about where you'll be and with whom and why it's important to you to stay out later . . . , they just might say yes."

Or if your parents want to screen your friends—as well they should—don't whimper like a child. Recommended *Seventeen* magazine: "Bring friends home with you from time to time, so that when you say you're going to the movies with Bill, your father has no reason to roar from the other room, 'Bill? Bill who?'"

"More Will Be Given"

Jim smiles when he talks about his younger brother Ron. "There's only 11 months difference between us," he says, "but our parents treated us so differently. They gave me a lot of freedom. I had the use of the family car. One year they even allowed me to take one younger brother on a trip to New York City.

"It was different with Ron, though," Jim continues. "He wasn't given much freedom at all. Dad didn't even bother teaching him how to drive when he came of age. And when he felt he was old enough to start dating, my folks wouldn't let him."

Favoritism? No. Explains Jim: "Ron tended to be irresponsible. He lacked initiative. He often failed to do what was assigned him. And although I *never* talked back to my parents, Ron would let them know he disagreed. This invariably backfired on him." Jesus said at Matthew 25:29: "For to everyone that has, more will be given and he will have abundance; but as for him that does not have, even what he has will be taken away from him."

Do you want more freedom and responsibility? Then prove yourself responsible. Take seriously whatever tasks your folks assign you. Don't be like the youth in one of Jesus' parables. After being told by his father, "Child, go work today in the vineyard," he said, "I will, sir," but he "did not go out." (Matthew 21:28, 29) Convince your parents that if they ask you to do something, no matter how small, it is as good as done.

"I showed my folks I could handle responsibility," Jim recalls. "They would send me to the bank, let me pay our utilities bills, go to the supermarket and shop. And when Mom had to go out and get a job, I even cooked the family meals."

Taking the Initiative

What if your parents simply haven't assigned you such tasks to do? Pursue various initiatives. *Seventeen* magazine suggested: "Offer to cook your family a meal, and tell your folks you want to do everything: plan the meal, make the grocery list, budget, shop, cook, clean up." And if cooking is not your forte, look around and see what else can be cared for. You don't need a specific decree from your parents to act when there are dishes to be washed, floors to be swept, or rooms to be straightened up.

Many youths take on part-time work during the summer or on weekends. If this is true in your case, have you proved that you are capable of *saving* and *managing* your money? Have you volunteered to make a contribution for your room and board? (You might find it *eye*-opening to check the going rate for renting a room in your community.) Doing so might mean less pocket money, but as your folks observe your grown-up way of handling money, they will no doubt be inclined to give you more freedom.

Loosening the Apron Strings

Parents should be our confidential friends, rich sources of advice and counsel. (Compare Jeremiah

3:4.) However, this does not mean that you must rely on them to make *every* petty decision. It is only through using your "perceptive powers" that you gain confidence in your ability to make decisions.—Hebrews 5:14.

So instead of running to your parents at the first sign of minor distress, try first to work out the problem in your own mind. Rather than be "overhasty," or impulsive, about matters, follow the Bible's advice to "consider knowledge" first. (Isaiah 32:4) Do some research, especially if Bible principles are involved. After calmly weighing matters, *then* approach your parents. Instead of always saying, 'Dad, what should I do?' or, 'Mom, what would you do?' explain the situation. Let them hear the way you have reasoned the situation out. Then ask for their observations.

Your parents now see you talking not as a child but as an adult. You have taken a big step toward proving that you are becoming an adult deserving of a measure of freedom. Your folks may very well begin to treat you like an adult.

Questions for Discussion   Chapter 3

☐ *Why are parents often so concerned about protecting their children and knowing their whereabouts?*

☐ *Why is it important that you treat your parents with respect?*

☐ *How can misunderstandings with your parents be best handled?*

☐ *How can you cooperate with your parents' rules and regulations and still have some freedom?*

☐ *What are some ways you can prove to your parents that you are responsible?*

Chapter 4

Why Did Dad and Mom Split Up?

"I remember when my dad left us. We really didn't know what was going on. Mom had to go to work and left us alone all the time. Sometimes we'd just sit by the window and worry whether she had left us too. . . . "
—*A girl from a divorced family.*

THE divorce of one's parents can seem like the end of the world, a catastrophe that generates enough misery to last forever. It often triggers an onslaught of feelings of shame, anger, anxiety, fear of abandonment, guilt, depression, and profound loss—even a desire for revenge.

If your parents have recently split up, you too might be experiencing such feelings. After all, our Creator meant for you to be raised by both a father and a mother. (Ephesians 6:1-3) Yet, now you have been deprived of the daily presence of a parent you love. "I really looked up to my father and wanted to be with him," laments Paul, whose folks split up when he was seven. "But Mom got custody of us."

Why Parents Break Up

Often parents have kept their problems well hidden. "I don't remember my folks fighting," says Lynn, whose parents divorced when she was a child. "I *thought* they got along." And even when parents do squabble, it may still come as a shock when they actually split up!

In many cases, the split-up occurs because one parent is guilty of sexual misconduct. God does

Watching the breakup of your parents' marriage can be one of the most painful experiences imaginable

permit the innocent mate to obtain a divorce. (Matthew 19:9) In other cases, "wrath and screaming and abusive speech" have erupted into violence, causing one parent to fear for his or her physical well-being and that of the children.—Ephesians 4:31.

Some divorces, admittedly, are obtained on flimsy grounds. Rather than work out their problems, some selfishly divorce because they claim they are 'unhappy' or 'no longer in love.' This is displeasing to God, who "has hated a divorcing." (Malachi 2:16) Jesus also indicated that some would break up their marriages because their mates became Christians. —Matthew 10:34-36.

Whatever the case, the fact that your parents may have chosen to be silent or to give you only vague answers to your questions regarding the divorce does not mean they do not love you.* Wrapped up in their own hurt, your parents may simply find it hard to talk about the divorce. (Proverbs 24:10) They may also find

---

* Researchers Wallerstein and Kelly discovered that "four-fifths of the youngest children [of divorced parents] studied were not provided with either an adequate explanation or assurance of continued care. In effect, they awoke one morning to find one parent gone."

'Will the Divorce Ruin My Life?'

In the wake of their parents' divorce, some youths virtually ruin their lives. Some make rash decisions, such as to quit school. Others vent their frustration and anger by misbehaving—as if to punish their parents for getting the divorce. Recalls Denny: "I was unhappy and depressed after my parents' divorce. I started having problems in school and failed one year. After that . . . I became the class clown and got into a lot of fights."

Shocking behavior may very well get the attention of one's parents. But what is really accomplished, other than adding stress to an already stressful situation? Really, the only one punished by wrongdoing is the wrongdoer. (Galatians 6:7) Try to understand that your parents are also suffering and that their seeming neglect of you is not malicious. Confessed Denny's mother: "I definitely neglected my kids. After the divorce, I was such a mess myself, I just couldn't help them."

The Bible advises at Hebrews 12:13: "Keep making straight paths for your feet, that what is lame may not be put out of joint." Even if parental discipline is absent, there is no excuse for misconduct. (James 4:17) Assume responsibility for your actions and exercise self-discipline. —1 Corinthians 9:27.

Avoid, too, making rash decisions, for example, to leave home. "The shrewd one considers his steps." (Proverbs 14:15) If your parents seem too distracted at this point to lend you their ear, why not talk your decisions over with an older friend?

Still, you may have a number of concerns about your future. Since your parents have failed at marriage, it's understandable that you might worry about your own prospect of enjoying a successful marriage. Fortunately, marital unhappiness is not something you inherit from your parents —like freckles. You are a unique individual, and how any future marriage of yours turns out will depend, not on your parents' failings, but on the extent to which you and your mate apply God's Word.

You may also find yourself worrying about things you formerly took for granted—food, clothing, shelter, money. Parents, however, usually work out some means of supporting their children after a divorce, even if Mom has to take on secular work. Nevertheless, the book Surviving the Breakup realistically warns: "What once supported one family unit must now support two families, forcing a decline in standard of living for every family member."

It may well be, therefore, that you'll have to get used to doing without things you used to enjoy, like new clothes. But the Bible reminds us: "We have brought nothing into the world, and neither can we carry anything out. So, having sustenance and covering, we shall be content with these things." (1 Timothy 6:7, 8) Perhaps you can even assist in working out a new family budget. Remember, too, that Jehovah is "a father of fatherless boys." (Psalm 68:5) You can be sure that he is deeply concerned about your needs.

Jeremiah observed: "Good it is for an able-bodied man that he should carry the yoke during his youth." (Lamentations 3:27) True, there is little "good" in watching parents split up. But it is possible to turn even this negative experience to your advantage.

Researcher Judith Wallerstein observed: "The emotional and intellectual growth [among children of divorced parents] that was catalyzed by the family crisis was impressive and sometimes moving. The youngsters . . . soberly considered their parents' experiences and drew thoughtful conclusions for their own futures. They were concerned with finding ways to avoid the mistakes their parents had made."

No doubt about it, your parents' breakup is sure to make its mark on your life. But whether that mark is a fading blemish or a festering wound is to a great extent up to you.

it awkward and embarrassing to admit to their mutual failures.

What You Can Do

Try to discern the right time to discuss calmly your concerns with your parents. (Proverbs 25:11) Let them know how saddened and confused you are over the divorce. Perhaps they will give you a satisfactory explanation. If not, do not despair. Did not Jesus withhold information that he felt his disciples were not ready to handle? (John 16:12) And do not your parents have a right to privacy?

Finally, appreciate that the divorce, whatever the reason for it, is a dispute between them—not with you! In their study of 60 divorced families, Wallerstein and Kelly found that couples blamed each other, their employers, family members, and friends for the divorce. But, say the researchers: "No one, interestingly enough, blamed the children." Your parents' feelings toward you are unchanged.

Dwelling on memories of how life used to be may only depress you

YOUNG PEOPLE ASK . . .

The Healing Effects of Time

There is "a time to heal." (Ecclesiastes 3:3) And just as a literal wound, like a broken bone, can take weeks or even months to heal completely, emotional wounds take time to heal.

Divorce researchers Wallerstein and Kelly found that within just a couple of years after a divorce "the widespread fears, the grief, the shocked disbelief . . . faded or disappeared altogether." Some experts feel that the worst of a divorce is over within just three years. This may seem like a long time, but a lot has to happen before your life can stabilize.

For one thing, the household routine—disrupted by the divorce—must be reorganized. Time will also pass before your parents are back on their feet emotionally. Only then may they finally be able to give you needed support. As your life regains some semblance of regularity, you will begin to feel normal again.

However, Solomon gave this warning: "Do not say: 'Why has it happened that the former days proved to be better than these?' for it is not due to wisdom that you have asked about this." (Ecclesiastes 7:10) Dwelling on the past can blind you to the present. What was your family situation like before the divorce? "There were always a lot of fights—screaming and name-calling," admits Annette. Could it be that you now enjoy domestic peace?

'I Can Get Them Back Together'

Some youths nurture dreams of reuniting their parents, perhaps clinging to such fantasies even after their parents have remarried!

However, denying the divorce changes nothing. And all the tears, pleading, and scheming in the world probably won't get your folks back together again. So why torment yourself by dwelling on the unlikely? (Proverbs 13:12) Solomon said that there is "a time to give up as lost." (Ecclesiastes 3:6) So accept both the reality and the permanence of the divorce. This is a big step toward your getting over it.

Coming to Terms With Your Parents

You may rightly be angry with your parents for disrupting your life. As one young man bitterly put it: "My parents were selfish. They didn't really think about us and how what they did would affect us. They just went ahead and made their plans." This may be true. But can you go through life carrying a load of anger and bitterness and not harm yourself?

The Bible counsels: "Let all malicious bitterness and anger and wrath . . . be taken away from you . . . But become kind to one another, tenderly compassionate, freely forgiving one another." (Ephesians 4:31, 32) How can you forgive someone who has hurt you so deeply? Try to view your parents objectively—as fallible, imperfect humans. Yes, even parents 'sin and fall short of the glory of God.' (Romans 3:23) Realizing this can help you come to terms with your parents.

Talk Out Your Feelings

"I've never really discussed how I felt about my parents' divorce," one young man said when interviewed by us. Though initially impassive, the youth became increasingly emotional—even tearful—as he spoke about his parents' divorce. Feelings that had long been buried were unearthed. Surprised at this, he confessed: "Talking it out really helped me."

You may likewise find it helpful to confide in someone, instead of isolating yourself. Let your parents know just how you feel, what your fears and anxieties are. (Compare Proverbs 23:26.) Mature Christians can

40   *YOUNG PEOPLE ASK . . .*

also help. Keith, for example, got little or no support from his family, which was torn apart by divorce. Yet he found support elsewhere. Says Keith: "The Christian congregation became my family."

Above all, you can find a hearing ear with your heavenly Father, the "Hearer of prayer." (Psalm 65:2) A youth named Paul recalls what helped him get over his parents' divorce: "I prayed all the time and always felt that Jehovah was a real person."

Getting On With Your Life

After a divorce, things may never be the same. This does not mean, though, that your life cannot be a fruitful and happy one. The Bible advises, "Do not loiter at your business." (Romans 12:11) Yes, instead of allowing yourself to become immobilized by grief, hurt, or anger, get on with your life! Get involved in your schoolwork. Pursue a hobby. Have "plenty to do in the work of the Lord."—1 Corinthians 15:58.

It will take work, determination, and the passing of time. But eventually the breakup of your parents' marriage will no longer be the dominant thing in your life.

Questions for Discussion   *Chapter 4*

□ *What are some of the reasons why parents break up?*

□ *Why might it be hard for your parents to talk about it? What can you do if they show such a reluctance to talk?*

□ *Why is it pointless to dwell on the past or fantasize about getting your parents back together again?*

□ *What are some positive things you can do to help yourself get over the divorce?*

□ *How can you deal with the anger you might feel toward your parents?*

How Can I Deal With My Parent's Remarriage?

"The day Dad married Rita was the worst day of my life," recalled Shane. "I was mad. Mad at Dad for being a traitor to my Mom. Mad at Mom for going off to law school and leaving us alone. Mad at the two brats, Rita's kids, who were going to come live in our house . . . But most of all, I was mad at Rita . . . I hated her. And because I believed it's not right to hate, I was mad at myself, too."—Stepfamilies—New Patterns in Harmony, by Linda Craven.

THE remarriage of a parent destroys the hope that your parents will ever get back together. It can make you feel insecure, betrayed, and jealous.

The remarriage can be particularly hurtful if it comes on the heels of the death of a beloved parent. "The death of my mother made me turn very bitter," admitted 16-year-old Missy. "I thought my father's fiancée was taking my mother's place so I was very mean to her." Loyal to your natural parent, you may even feel guilty if you begin to feel love toward a stepparent.

Little wonder, then, that many youths vent their emotional pain in destructive ways. Some even scheme to break up their parent's new marriage. But remember, your natural parent and stepparent have exchanged vows before God. "Therefore, what God has yoked together let no man [or child] put apart." (Matthew 19:6) And even if you could break them up, this would not reunite your natural parents.

YOUNG PEOPLE ASK . . .

A parent's remarriage often ignites feelings of anger, insecurity, and jealousy

Nor does it make any sense to be in constant conflict with a stepparent. Proverbs 11:29 warns: "He who brings trouble on his family will inherit only wind," that is, end up with nothing. (*New International Version*) Fifteen-year-old Gerri's resentment of her stepmother finally culminated in a bitter fight. The result? Her stepmother demanded that Gerri's father choose between her and his daughter. Gerri ended up moving back in with her natural mother—who had also remarried.

Love Helps You Cope

What is the secret to coping successfully with a parent's remarriage? Exercising principled love as described at 1 Corinthians 13:4-8:

Love *"does not look for its own interests."* This means 'seeking not our own advantage, but that of the other person.' (1 Corinthians 10:24) If a parent has decided that he or she again needs the companionship of a marriage partner, should you resent this?

"Love *is not jealous."* Often youths do not want to share their natural parent's love with anyone else. But you need not fear that your parent will run out of love, as love can expand. (Compare 2 Corinthians 6:11-13.) Your natural parent can expand his or her love to include a new mate without losing any affection for you! Will you open your heart to include a stepparent? Doing so in no way means that you are disloyal to your departed parent.

Love *"does not behave indecently."* Living with new brothers or sisters of the opposite sex can create moral pressures. Reportedly, illicit sexual relations take place among family members in 25 percent of stepfamilies.

Says David, whose mother's remarriage brought four teenage stepsisters into the house, "It was necessary to put up a mental block concerning sexual feelings." You will also want to be careful to avoid undue familiarity, making sure that neither your dress nor your behavior is sexually provocative.—Colossians 3:5.

Love *"bears up under anything . . . It gives us power to endure in anything."* (Charles B. Williams' translation) At times nothing seems to make your painful feelings go away! Marla admitted: "I felt that I had no place in the home. I even told my mom that I wished I had never been born." Marla rebelled and even ran away! However, she now says: "The best thing is to endure." If you likewise endure, in time the bitterness, bewilderment, and pain you initially felt will subside.

'You're Not My Real Mother/Father!'

Coming under the discipline of a new parent is not easy, and when asked to do something by a stepparent, it may be tempting to blurt out, 'You're not my real mother/father!' But recall the principle stated at 1 Corinthians 14:20: "Grow up in your thinking."—*The Holy Bible in the Language of Today,* by William Beck.

Accepting the authority of your stepparent to discipline you is one way to show that you have 'grown up in your thinking.' He or she performs the duties of a natural parent and deserves your respect. (Proverbs 1:8; Ephesians 6:1-4) In Bible times Esther was reared by an adoptive father, or "caretaker," when her parents died. Though he was not her natural parent,

> **"I** thought my father's fiancée was taking my mother's place so I was very mean to her"

Mordecai 'laid commandments on her,' which she obeyed even as an adult! (Esther 2:7, 15, 17, 20) Really, a stepparent's discipline is usually an expression of his or her love and concern for you.—Proverbs 13:24.

Still, legitimate complaints are bound to occur. If so, prove yourself to be 'grown up' by doing as Colossians 3:13 urges: "Continue putting up with one another and forgiving one another freely if anyone has a cause for complaint against another."

Learn to Share, Learn to Compromise

When 15-year-old Jamie lived alone with her mother, she had her own room and wore expensive clothes. When her mother remarried and Jamie found herself in a family with four children, things changed. "Now I don't even have my own room anymore," she lamented. "I have to share everything."

You may also have to relinquish your position as the oldest or the only child. If you are a son, for a long time you may have served as the man of the house—a position now occupied by your stepfather. Or if you are a daughter, it may be that you and your mother were like sisters, even sleeping in the same room, but now you have been moved out by your stepdad.

"Let your reasonableness become known to all

Discipline from a stepparent is often resented

men," recommends the Bible. (Philippians 4:5) The original word used meant "yielding" and conveyed the spirit of one who did not insist on all his lawful rights. So, try to be yielding, compromising. Make the most of your new situation, and avoid dwelling on the past. (Ecclesiastes 7:10) Be willing to share with stepbrothers and stepsisters, not treating them as outsiders. (1 Timothy 6:18) The sooner you begin treating one another as real brothers and sisters, the sooner your feelings for one another will grow. And as for the new man of the house, don't resent him. Be glad that he is there to help carry the load of household responsibilities.

Coping With Unequal Treatment

After admitting that her stepfather shows love, one young girl added: "But there is a difference. He expects more, disciplines more, has less understanding towards us . . . than he does of his own children at the same age. This is a sore spot with us."

Realize that a stepparent usually will not feel the same way toward a stepchild as he does toward his natural one. This is due, not so much to the blood tie with his natural child, but to their shared experience in living. After all, even a blood-related parent may love one child more than another. (Genesis 37:3) There is, however, an important distinction between equal and fair. People have individual personalities and differing needs. So instead of being overly concerned about whether you are treated equally, try to see if your stepparent is striving to meet your needs. If you feel that these are not being met, then you have reason to discuss the matter with your stepparent.

Your stepbrothers or stepsisters can also be a source of contention. Never forget that they too may be having a hard time adjusting to the stepfamily situation. Perhaps they even resent you as an intrusion into their family. So do your best to be kind. If they snub you, try 'conquering evil with good.' (Romans 12:21) Besides, it is nothing strange even for biological brothers and sisters to clash from time to time.—See Chapter 6.

Patience Pays Off!

"Better is the end afterward of a matter than its beginning. Better is one who is patient than one who is haughty in spirit." (Ecclesiastes 7:8) Normally, several years are needed before trust develops to the point where members of a stepfamily feel at ease with one another. Only then may diverse habits and values blend into a workable routine. So be patient! Do not expect to experience "instant love" or that an "instant family" will result.

When Thomas' mother remarried, he was uneasy, to say the least. His mother had four children, and the man she married had three. "We had fights, arguments, disruptions, terrible emotional strains," wrote Thomas. What brought eventual success? "By applying Bible principles, things were resolved; not always immediately, but with time and the application of the fruits of God's spirit, situations were eventually smoothed over." —Galatians 5:22, 23.

That a commitment to Bible principles really brings

about success in a stepfamily is illustrated by the experiences of the following youths whom we interviewed:

Youths in Successful Stepfamilies

Interviewer: How did you avoid resenting your stepparent's discipline?

Lynch: My mother and stepfather always stood together on discipline. When something happened, they both came to a decision to do it, so when I got a spanking, I knew it was from both.

Linda: It was very hard at first because I would say, "What right do you have to tell me this?" But then I thought of how the Bible says to 'Honor your mother and father.' Even though he was not my natural father, in God's sight he was still my father.

Robin: I knew that it would deeply hurt my mother for me to resent the person she loved.

Interviewer: What promoted good communication?

Lynch: You have to get interested in what your stepparent does. I helped him at his secular work. And as we worked we would talk and talk. This helped me to see how he thought. Other times I would just sit with him, and we would talk about 'nothing.'

Valerie: My stepmother and I spent a lot of time together, and I really got to understand her. We became the closest of friends.

Robin: My father died just a year before Mom's remarriage. I refused to get close to my stepfather because I didn't want him to replace my father. I prayed that God would help me get over my father's death and get closer to my stepdad. I prayed and prayed and prayed. Jehovah really answered these prayers.

Interviewer: What did you do to get closer?

Valerie: Sometimes I would ask my stepmom to go

to a show with me—just the two of us. Or when I was out, I would buy her some flowers or a vase, something to show her that I was thinking about her. She really appreciated this.

Eric: You have to search for something you both enjoy. The only thing that I had in common with my stepfather was that he was married to my mother and we lived in the same house. The biggest help came when I began to take the same interest in the Bible that he had. As I drew closer to Jehovah God, I got much closer to my stepfather. Now we really had something in common!

Interviewer: How have you personally benefited?

Robin: When I lived just with my mother, I was rebellious and spoiled. I always wanted things my way. Now I've learned to consider others and be more unselfish.

Lynch: My stepfather helped me think like a man. He's helped me gain skills and know how to use my hands. When times were rough and I needed someone, he was there. Yes, he's the best father that anyone could ever have had.

Questions for Discussion
Chapter 5

□ *How do many youths feel when their parents remarry? Why?*

□ *How does showing Christian love help a youth cope?*

□ *Do you have to submit to the discipline of a stepparent?*

□ *Why is it important to know how to compromise and share?*

□ *Should you expect equal treatment with stepbrothers and stepsisters? What if you feel you are being treated unfairly?*

□ *What are some things you can do that will help you get along better with a stepparent?*

Chapter 6

Why Are My Brother and Sister So Hard to Get Along With?

SIBLING rivalry—it's as old as Cain and Abel. Not that you hate your sibling (brother or sister). One youth admitted: "Deep down in my heart, where I cannot feel it now, I guess I love my brother. Sort of, I do."

Why does animosity so often lurk beneath the surface of sibling relationships? Writer Harriet Webster quotes family therapist Claudia Schweitzer as saying: "Each family has a certain amount of resources, some emotional and some material." Adds Webster: "When sibs fight, they're usually competing for these resources, which includes everything from parental love to money and clothes." Camille and her five brothers and sisters, for example, share three bedrooms. "I want to be by myself sometimes," Camille says, "and I'll want to shut them out, but they're always there."

Battle lines may also be drawn over sharing privileges and household responsibilities. Older youngsters may resent being expected to do the lion's share of the chores. Younger children may balk at being bossed by an older sibling or may become jealous when older siblings receive coveted privileges. 'My sister takes driving lessons and I can't,' laments a teenage girl from England. 'I feel resentful and try to make things difficult for her.'

Sometimes sibling discord is simply the result of personality clashes. Seventeen-year-old Diane says of her siblings: "If you see one another every single day, day in and day out . . . And if you watch the same person every day do the same thing that annoys you—that can get to you." Young Andre adds: "When you're at home . . . , you act the way you really are." Unfortunately, 'acting the way you really are' often means dispensing with politeness, kindness, and tact.

Parental preferences ('Mom likes you best!') are another common bone of contention between siblings. Admits professor of psychology Lee Salk: "There's no way a parent can love all her children exactly the same because they are different human beings and inevitably elicit different reactions from us [parents]." This was true in Bible times. The patriarch Jacob (Israel) "loved Joseph more than all his other sons." (Genesis 37:3) Joseph's brothers came to be bitterly jealous of him.

Putting Out the Fire

"Where there is no wood the fire goes out." So says Proverbs 26:20. The spread of forest fires is often prevented by the cutting of firebreaks, strips of land where all the trees have been cut down. If a fire does start, it usually advances only to that point and then dies out. Similarly, there are ways to prevent—or at least limit—disagreements. One way is to communicate and work out a compromise before an argument flares up.

For example, is the problem a lack of privacy? If so, at a time when the issue is not raging, try sitting down together and working out an actual schedule. ('I get the room to myself on these days/hours, and you get it on these.') Then "let your word *Yes* mean Yes, your *No*, No" by respecting the agreement. (Matthew 5:37) If something comes up that calls for an adjustment, let the other person know in advance, instead of just thrusting the change upon him or her without notice.

Are you battling over property rights? One teenager complained: "My stepsister always uses my things without asking me. She even used my makeup, and then had the nerve to tell me I didn't buy the right kind!" You could call upon your parents as the final arbiters. But better yet, sit down with your brother or sister at a calm moment. Rather than quibble over personal "rights," be "ready to share." (1 Timothy 6:18) Try to agree upon some rules regarding borrowing, one of which might be always to ask before taking. Work out compromises if necessary. In this way you can watch the 'fire go out' before it starts!

> "*There's no way a parent can love all her children exactly the same because they are different human beings.*"
> —Professor of psychology Lee Salk

But what if a sibling's personality simply rubs you the wrong way? Really, you can do little to change that one. So learn to 'put up with one another in love.' (Ephesians 4:2) Instead of magnifying a sibling's faults and flaws, apply Christian love, which "covers a multitude of sins." (1 Peter 4:8) Instead of being abrasive or unkind, put away "wrath, anger, badness, abusive speech," and "let your utterance be always with graciousness."—Colossians 3:8; 4:6.

'It's Not Fair!'

"My sister gets everything she wants," laments one youth. "But when it comes to me, I get left out completely." Sound familiar? But note those two absolutes, "everything" and "completely." Is the situation really that dire? Not likely. And even if it is, is it realistic to expect absolutely equal treatment for two different individuals? Of course not! Your parents may simply be responding to your individual needs and temperaments.

But isn't it unfair for parents to favor a particular child? Not necessarily. Recall how Jacob favored his son Joseph. The reason? Joseph was the son of Jacob's beloved wife Rachel, who had died. Is it not perfectly understandable that Jacob felt especially close to this son? Jacob's love for Joseph, however, did not exclude his other sons, as he expressed real concern for their welfare. (Genesis 37: 13, 14) Their jealousy of Joseph was thus unfounded!

Your parents may similarly be drawn to your brother or to your sister, perhaps because of shared interests, similar

I often miss not having a sister; yet I do have certain advantages

'*I*'m an Only Child'

If this is your situation, you are not necessarily disadvantaged. For one thing, while other youths may have difficulty getting along with their siblings, you can hand pick your close companions (with your parents' approval, of course). You may even have more time for study, meditation, or the development of certain skills or talents.—See Chapter 14 on loneliness.

Young Thomas points to another advantage when he says: "As an only child I had the total attention of my parents." True, excessive parental attention can make a youth self-centered. But if parents show balance in rendering it, parental attention can help you to mature more quickly and to feel at ease around adults.

Since you do not have brothers or sisters to share things with, however, there is the danger of being selfish. Jesus advised: "Practice giving." (Luke 6:38) Try sharing things with friends and relatives. Develop an eye for the needs of others, offering your help where possible. People will respond to such generosity. And you may find that although you are an only child, you are far from a lonely one.

personality, or other factors. This does not mean that they do not love you. If you feel resentment or jealousy, realize that your imperfect heart has simply got the better of you. Work to overcome such feelings. As long as your needs are being met, why become disturbed if a sibling seems to get extra attention?

Brothers and Sisters—A Blessing

This may seem hard to believe at times—especially when they are annoying you. But young Diane reminds us: "It's fun having brothers and sisters." She has seven. "You have someone to talk to and share your interests with."

Anne Marie and her brother Andre add: "Even though you can go places with your friends, you always have your brothers and sisters. They are always there when you want to play a game or sport or go to the park." Donna sees another practical advantage: "You have someone to share the chores with." Others have described their brother or sister as "a special adviser and listener" and someone who "understands."

Later in life, you will experience some of the very same problems with others that you now have with your brother or sister. Jealousy, property rights, unequal treatment, lack of privacy, selfishness, personality differences—such problems are a part of life. Learning to get along with your brothers and sisters is good training in the field of human relations.

Seventeen-year-old Andre echoes the Bible's words at 1 John 4:20 when he says: "If you can't get along with people you can see, how can you get along with Jehovah, whom you can't see?" Disagreements with your brothers and sisters will occur from time to time. But you can learn to share, communicate, and compromise. The result of such effort? You may well decide that having a brother or a sister isn't so bad after all.

Questions for Discussion   *Chapter 6*

☐ *Why do brothers and sisters often clash?*

☐ *How can you prevent fights over privacy and property rights?*

☐ *Why do parents sometimes favor a particular child? Do you feel this is necessarily unfair?*

☐ *Is an only child disadvantaged?*

☐ *What are some advantages of having brothers and sisters?*

Chapter 7

Should I Leave Home?

"Mom & Dad:

"Well I'm finally leaving. As I've said before, I'm not doing this to spite you or get back at you in any way. I cannot be happy being confined like you want me to be. Maybe I won't be happy this way either, but I'd just like to find out."

THUS began a 17-year-old girl's farewell letter to her parents. In the Federal Republic of Germany, for example, every third girl and every fourth boy between the ages of 15 and 24 now lives away from home. Perhaps you have thought about leaving home yourself.

God foresaw that the desire to marry would cause a person to "leave his father and his mother." (Genesis 2: 23, 24) And there are other valid reasons for leaving, such as expanding one's service to God. (Mark 10: 29, 30) For many youths, however, leaving home is simply a way of getting out of what they feel is an intolerable situation. Says one young man: "It's simply that you want to be more independent. Living at home with your parents is no longer satisfying. You are always getting into arguments, and they do not understand your needs. Besides, you feel so restricted, always having to answer to your parents for your every move."

Ready for Independence?

But does the fact that you desire independence mean that you are ready for it? For one thing, making it on your own may not be as easy as you think. Jobs are often scarce. Rents have skyrocketed. And what are youths caught in an economic bind often forced to do? Say the authors of *Pulling Up Roots:* "They return home and expect parents to reassume the burden of their support."

And what about your mental, emotional, and spiritual maturity? You may fancy yourself to be a grown-up, but your parents may still see in you some of "the traits of a babe." (1 Corinthians 13:11) And really, are not your parents in the best position to judge how much freedom you are ready to handle? To go against their judgment and set out on your own could invite disaster! —Proverbs 1:8.

'I Don't Get Along With My Folks!'

Is this true in your case? Even so, this is no reason to start packing your bags. As a youth, you still need your parents and will likely benefit from their insight and wisdom for years to come. (Proverbs 23:22) Should you cut them out of your life just because you have run into a few snags in dealing with them?

> "**N**ever leave home just because you can't get along with your parents . . . how will you ever be able to get along with other people?"

A young German named Karsten who left home to pursue a career as a full-time minister puts it this way: "Never leave home just because you can't get along with your parents. If you can't get along with them, how will you ever be able to get along with other people? Moving out will not solve your problem. To the contrary, it will only prove you are too immature to stand on your own feet and will lead to greater estrangement from your parents."

Morals and Motives

Youths also tend to overlook the moral dangers involved in leaving home prematurely. In Luke 15:

11-32, Jesus tells of a young man who wanted to be independent and set out on his own. No longer under the good influence of his parents, he began "living a debauched life," succumbing to sexual immorality. Soon he had squandered his finances. Employment was so hard to come by that he even took a job that Jews despised—herding pigs. The so-called prodigal, or wasteful, son came to his senses, however. Swallowing his pride, he returned home and begged his father for forgiveness.

Although this parable was told to highlight God's mercy, it also contains this practical lesson: Leaving home with an unwise motive can harm you morally and spiritually! Sad to say, some Christian youths embarking on an independent course have suffered spiritual ruin. Unable to stay afloat financially, some have resorted to sharing expenses with other youths whose life-style conflicts with Bible principles.—1 Corinthians 15:33.

A German youth named Horst recalls a youth his own age who left home: "Although not married, he began living with his girl friend. They had parties where liquor flowed freely, and he often ended up getting drunk. Had he still been living at home, his parents would have allowed none of this." Horst concluded: "It's true, once you leave home you have more freedom. But to be completely honest, is it not oftentimes used as an opportunity to do bad things?"

So if you yearn for more freedom, ask yourself: Just why do I want greater freedom? Is it so that I can have material possessions or leeway to act in ways my parents would forbid if I lived at home? Remember what the Bible says at Jeremiah 17:9: "The heart is more treacherous than anything else and is desperate. Who can know it?"

YOUNG PEOPLE ASK . . .

How Can I Grow Up if I Don't Move Out?

The book *Adolescence* observes: "Simply moving out of the family home does not guarantee a successful transition [to adulthood]. Nor does staying at home imply the failure to grow up." Indeed, growing up means more than having one's own money, job, and apartment. For one thing, life is mastered by facing problems squarely. Nothing is gained by running away from situations that are not to our liking. "Good it is for an able-bodied man that he should carry the yoke during his youth," says Lamentations 3:27.

Take, for example, parents who are hard to get along with or are very strict. Mac, now 47 years old, had a father who saddled him with afterschool chores. During summer vacation, while other youths played, Mac had to work. "I thought he was the meanest man alive for keeping us from playing and enjoying ourselves,"

The domestic skills needed to live on one's own can be learned at home

Is Running Away the Answer?

Over a million teenagers run away from home each year. Some are running from intolerable situations—such as physical or sexual abuse. But more often than not, running away is sparked by arguments with parents over such matters as curfews, school grades, household chores, and choice of friends.

Perhaps your parents' outlook and thinking on matters simply does not coincide with yours. But have you considered the fact that your parents are obligated before God to bring you up "in the discipline and mental-regulating of Jehovah"? (Ephesians 6:4) So they may insist that you accompany them to religious meetings and activities or even restrict your association with other youths. (1 Corinthians 15:33) Is that any reason to rebel or run away? You too have an obligation before God: "Honor your father and your mother." —Ephesians 6:1-3.

Besides, running away solves nothing. "Running away only

creates more problems for you," reflects Amy, who ran away at age 14. Says Margaret O. Hyde in her book <u>My Friend Wants to Run Away</u>: "A few runaways actually get jobs and make it on their own. But, for most of them, life is worse than it was before they left home." And notes 'Teen magazine: "Teens don't find freedom on the streets. Instead, they find other runaways or throwaways—like themselves—living in abandoned buildings, where they have no protection from rapists or muggers. They also find a lot of people who make it their dirty business to exploit young people, and teenage runaways are an easy target."

As a runaway, Amy was "befriended" by a 22-year-old male, who made her pay for her stay "by having sex with him and nine of his friends." She also "got drunk and took lots of drugs." Another girl, named Sandi, suffered molestation by her foster grandfather and ran away. She

became a prostitute living on the streets and sleeping on park benches or wherever she could. They are typical of many runaways.

Most runaways have few salable skills. Neither do they usually have any of the necessary paperwork to get hired: birth certificate, Social Security card, permanent address. "I've had to steal, to panhandle," says Luis, "but mainly steal because nobody gives you nothing out there." Some 60 percent of the runaways are girls, many of whom support themselves by prostitution. Pornographers, drug dealers, and pimps frequent the bus stations looking for runaways to exploit. They may offer scared youths a place to sleep and food to eat. They may even give them what they lacked at home—a feeling that they are loved.

In time, though, such "benefactors" demand payment. And that could mean working for them as a prostitute, engaging in sexual perversions, or posing for pornographic pictures. Little wonder that many runaways end up seriously injured—or dead!

It thus makes sense to put forth every effort—and that means more than once—to talk with your parents. Let them know how you feel and what is going on. (See Chapters 2 and 3.) In cases of physical or sexual abuse, outside help may be needed.

Whatever the case, talk, don't run away. Even if life at home is not ideal, keep in mind that things can be even worse when you are on the run.

says Mac. "Often I thought, 'If only I could get away from here and have my own place!'" Mac, however, now has a different perspective on the matter: "What Dad did for me was priceless. He taught me how to do hard work and endure hardship. Since then I've had far more serious problems to face, but I know how to face them head on."

A Fool's Paradise

Simply living at home, however, does not guarantee your maturing. Says one youth: "Living at home with my folks was like living in a fool's paradise. They did everything for me." Part of growing up is learning how to do things for yourself. Granted, taking out the garbage or doing the laundry is not as much fun as playing your favorite records. But what can result if you never learn how to do these things? You can become a helpless adult, thoroughly dependent upon your parents or others.

Are you (whether a young man or a young woman) preparing for eventual independence by learning how to cook, clean, iron, or make household or automotive repairs?

Economic Independence

Youths in affluent lands often view money as easy to come by and even easier to spend. If they have a part-time job, they are often prone to spend their cash on stereos and designer clothes. What a rude awakening such youths are in for, though, when they move out on their own! Recalls Horst (previously mentioned): "By the end of the month [out on my own] both my wallet and my cupboard were empty."

Why not learn how to handle money while you are living at home? Your parents have had years of experience doing this and can help you avoid many pitfalls. The book *Pulling Up Roots* suggests asking them such questions as: 'How much does it cost each month for electricity? Heat? Water? Telephone? What kind of taxes do we pay? What rent do we pay?' You may be shocked to learn that working youths often have more pocket money than their parents have! So if you have a job, offer to make a reasonable contribution to the upkeep of the household.

Learn Before You Leave

No, you do not need to leave home to grow up. But you must work hard while there to develop good judgment and levelheadedness. Learn, too, how to get along with others. Prove that you can take criticism, failure, or disappointment. Cultivate 'kindness, goodness, mildness, and self-control.' (Galatians 5:22, 23) These traits are the true marks of a grown Christian man or woman.

Sooner or later, circumstances, such as marriage, may well propel you out of the nest of your parents' home. But until then, why be in a big hurry to leave? Talk it over with your folks. They may be happy to have you stay, especially if you make a real contribution to the welfare of the family. With their help, you can continue growing, learning, and maturing right there at home.

Questions for Discussion　　　　　　　　　*Chapter 7*

□ *Why are many youths anxious to leave home?*

□ *Why are most youths unready for such a move?*

□ *What are some of the dangers in leaving home prematurely?*

□ *What are some of the problems faced by runaways?*

□ *How is it possible for you to mature while still living at home?*

You and Your Peers

Everybody needs friends. But when you are young, friends can have more influence over how you dress, act, and think than your parents do. Who, then, should be your friends? And to what extent should your life be molded by their opinions?

Chapter 8

How Can I Make Real Friends?

"I'VE been going to school in this district for eight years, but in all that time I've never managed to make one single friend! Not one." So lamented a youth named Ronny. And perhaps at times you have similarly felt like a failure at friendship. But just what are real friends? And what is the secret of having them?

A proverb says: "A friend is loving at all times and becomes a brother in times of trouble." (Proverbs 17: 17, *The Bible in Basic English*) But there is more to friendship than having a shoulder to cry on. Says a young woman named Marvia: "Sometimes a so-called friend will see you get into trouble and then say, 'I saw you leading up to that, but I was afraid to tell you.' But when a real friend sees you going the wrong way, she will try to warn you before it's too late—even if she knows you may not like what she says."

Would you allow a bruised ego to cause you to reject someone who has cared enough about you to tell you the truth? Proverbs 27:6 says: "There is more trust to be put in bruises from one who loves than in effusive kisses from one who hates." (*Byington*) A person who thinks straight and talks straight is thus the kind of person you should want as a friend.

Counterfeit Versus Real Friends

"My life is proof that not all 'friends' bring out your best," states 23-year-old Peggy. As a teenager, Peggy had been forced to leave home. She was befriended, however, by two of Jehovah's Witnesses, Bill and his wife, Lloy. They began a study of the Bible with Peggy. "The months I spent with them were filled with real joy, contentment and peace," said Peggy. Yet, she opted to be with some youths she had met—and left Bill and Lloy.

> **"I learned many things from my new 'friends' —stealing stereos, cashing bad checks, smoking marijuana and, finally, how to support a $200-a-day drug habit"**

Peggy further recounts: "I learned many things from my new 'friends'—stealing stereos, cashing bad checks, smoking marijuana and, finally, how to support a $200-a-day drug habit." At age 18 she met a young man named Ray who offered her all the drugs she could use—free. "I thought all my troubles were over. Never again would I have to steal and cheat," thought Peggy. Ray, however, introduced her to prostitution. Eventually Peggy fled the city and her fast-lane "friends."

At her new location, one day Peggy was visited by two of Jehovah's Witnesses. "Tears of joy flooded my eyes as I embraced the two startled women," related Peggy. "I had grown to despise the hypocrisy of my former 'friends,' but here were people who were for real." Peggy resumed her study of the Bible.

Conforming her life to God's ways, though, was not easy. Particularly difficult was giving up smoking. However, a Witness friend advised: "Instead of praying and asking for forgiveness after you fail, why not pray beforehand and ask for strength when you feel the urge to smoke?" Says Peggy: "This kind and practical suggestion did it. . . . For the first time in years, I felt clean inside and knew what it meant to have self-respect."

Peggy's experience highlights the truthfulness of the Bible's words at Proverbs 13:20: "He that is walking with wise persons will become wise, but he that is having dealings with the stupid ones will fare badly." Says Peggy: "If I had just kept my friendship with those persons who loved God, I would have avoided all those things that are now an ugly memory."

Finding Friends

Where can you find friends who love God? Within the Christian congregation. Search out youths who not only make a profession of faith but also have works to back up their faith and devotion. (Compare James 2:26.) If such youths are hard to find, get to know some Christians who are older than you. Age need not be a barrier to friendship. The Bible tells of the model friendship between David and Jonathan—and Jonathan was old enough to be David's father!—1 Samuel 18:1.

How, though, can you get friendships started?

An Active Interest in Others

Jesus Christ built friendships that were so strong that his friends were willing to die for him. Why? For

*D*o you have trouble making friends?

Should I Tell On My Friend?

If you became aware that a friend was dabbling in drugs, experimenting with sex, cheating, or stealing—would you tell someone responsible about it? Most would not, adhering to a peculiar code of silence that often prevails among youths.

Some fear being labeled a "squealer." Others have a misguided sense of loyalty. Viewing discipline as something harmful, they imagine they do their friend a favor by covering up his problems. Further, breaking that code of silence could expose one to the ridicule of peers and the possible loss of their friendship.

Nevertheless, when a youth named Lee learned that his best friend, Chris, was smoking, he decided to act. Says Lee: "My conscience was eating me up because I knew I had to tell someone!" A youth in Bible times was faced with a similar situation. "Joseph, when seventeen years old, happened to be tending sheep with his brothers . . . So Jo-seph brought a bad report about them to their father." (Genesis 37:2) Joseph knew that if he remained silent, the spiritual welfare of his brothers would be endangered.

Sin is a decaying, corrupting force. Unless an erring friend receives help—perhaps in the form of firm Scriptural discipline—he or she may plunge yet deeper into wickedness. (Ecclesiastes 8:11) Consequently, covering up a friend's wrongdoing not only does little good but also may do irreparable harm.

The Bible therefore exhorts: "Brothers, even though a man takes some false step before he is aware of it, you who have spiritual qualifications try to readjust such a man in a spirit of mildness." (Galatians 6:1) You may not feel you have the spiritual qualifications to readjust an erring friend. But would it not make sense to see to it that the matter is reported to someone who is qualified to help?

It is thus imperative that you approach your friend and lay bare his fault. (Compare Matthew 18:15.) This will take courage and boldness on your part. Be firm, giving convincing evidence regarding his sin, specifically telling what you know and how you came to know it. (Compare John 16:8.) Do not promise you won't tell anyone, for such a promise would be invalid in the eyes of God, who condemns covering up wrongdoing.—Proverbs 28:13.

Perhaps some misunderstanding has occurred. (Proverbs 18:13) If not, and wrongdoing is really involved, it may be that your friend is relieved to have his problem out in the open. Be a good listener. (James 1:19) Do not stifle the free flow of his feelings by using judgmental expressions, such as, "You shouldn't have!" or expressions of shock, such as, "How could you!" Show empathy and feel what your friend feels.—1 Peter 3:8.

Often the situation requires more help than you are in a position to give. Insist, then, that your friend reveal the wrong to his parents or other responsible adults. And if your friend refuses to do so? Let him know that if he does not clear up the matter within a reasonable period of time, you, as his true friend, will be obliged to go to someone in his behalf.—Proverbs 17:17.

At first your friend may not understand why you took such action. He may even become upset and rashly terminate your friendship. But says Lee: "I know I did the right thing by telling somebody. My conscience felt so much better because Chris was getting the help he needed. Later he came and told me that he was not upset with me for doing what I did and that also put me at ease."

If your acquaintance continues to resent your courageous actions, obviously he or she never was a true friend in the first place. But you will have the satisfaction of knowing that you proved your loyalty to God and showed yourself to be a true friend.

Taking an interest in others is the key to starting friendships

one thing, Jesus cared for people. He reached out and helped others. He 'wanted to' get involved. (Matthew 8:3) Truly, having an interest in others is the first step toward making friends.

A youth named David, for example, says he has had success in making friends because of "having a real love for people and taking an active interest in others." He adds: "One of the biggest things is to know the person's name. Others are often impressed that you cared enough to remember their name. Because of this they may share some experience or problem with you and the friendship starts to build."

This does not mean that you have to be a hand-pumping extrovert. Jesus was "lowly in heart," not flamboyant or showy. (Matthew 11:28, 29) It is sincere interest in others that attracts them. Often the simplest things, such as sharing a meal together or assisting someone with a task, can serve to deepen a friendship.

"How You Listen"

"Pay attention to how you listen," recommended Jesus. (Luke 8:18) Though he had in mind the value of listening to God's sayings, the principle applies well in developing relationships. Being a good listener is vital in building a friendship.

If we are genuinely interested in what others are saying, they are usually drawn to us. But this requires your "keeping an eye, not in personal interest upon just your own matters [perhaps on just what you want to say], but also in personal interest upon those of the others."—Philippians 2:4.

Be Loyal

Jesus stuck with his friends. He "loved them to the end." (John 13:1) A young man named Gordon treats his friends similarly: "The main quality of a friend is his loyalty. Will he really stick with you when times get rough? My friend and I would defend each other when others would say some belittling remarks. We really stuck up for each other—but only if we were in the right."

Counterfeit friends, though, think nothing of hypocritically stabbing one another in the back. "There exist companions disposed to break one another to pieces," says Proverbs 18:24. Would you "break" a friend's reputation by joining in vicious gossip, or would you loyally stand up for him?

Share Your Feelings

Jesus further endeared himself to others by revealing his deepest feelings. At times he let it be known that he "felt pity," "felt love," or was "deeply grieved." On at least one occasion he even "gave way to tears." Jesus was not embarrassed to lay bare his heart to those whom he trusted.—Matthew 9:36; 26:38; Mark 10:21; John 11:35.

This, of course, does not mean that you should pour

out your emotions to everyone that you meet! But you can be honest with everyone. And as you get to know and trust someone, you can gradually reveal more of your deepest feelings. At the same time, learning to have empathy and "fellow feeling" for others is essential for meaningful friendships.—1 Peter 3:8.

Do Not Expect Perfection

Even when a friendship is off to a good start, don't expect perfection. "We all make mistakes in all kinds of ways, but the man who can claim that he never says the wrong thing can consider himself perfect." (James 3:2, *Phillips*) Furthermore, friendship costs—time and emotion. "You have to be willing to give," says a young man named Presley. "That's a large part of friendship. You have your own feelings about things but you're willing to give in to make room for your friend's feelings and opinions."

The cost of friendship, however, is nothing compared to the cost of not loving—a life of empty loneliness. So make friends for yourself. (Compare Luke 16:9.) Give of yourself. Listen to and show a genuine interest in others. Like Jesus, you may then have numerous ones to whom you can say, "You are my friends."—John 15:14.

Questions for Discussion   *Chapter 8*

□ *How can you recognize a real friend? What kind of friends are counterfeit?*

□ *Where can you look for friends? Must they always be your age?*

□ *What should you do if a friend is in serious trouble?*

□ *What are four ways to make friends?*

Chapter 9

How Can I Cope With Peer Pressure?

AT THE age of 14, Karen was already a heavy drug user and regularly engaged in sex. By age 17, Jim was a confirmed alcoholic and living an immoral life. Both admit they did not really like the life they were living nor the things they were doing. Why, then, did they act as they did? *Peer pressure!*

"Everyone I was with was into these things, and that had a big effect on me," explains Karen. Jim agreed, saying, "I didn't want to lose my friends by being different."

Why Youths Follow Their Peers

As some youths get older, the influence of parents wanes, and a desire to be popular and to be accepted by peers grows strong. Others simply feel a need to talk with someone who "understands" or who will make them feel loved or needed. When such communication is lacking at home—as is often the case—they seek it among their peers. Often, too, a lack of self-confidence and feelings of insecurity cause some to be vulnerable to peer influence.

Peer influence is not necessarily bad. A proverb says: "By iron, iron itself is sharpened. So one man sharpens the face of another." (Proverbs 27:17) Just as an iron knife can sharpen the dulled edge of another knife, fellowship with other youths can 'sharpen' your personality and make you a better person—if those peers have mature, healthy attitudes.

All too often, though, youths are sadly lacking in maturity—both mental and spiritual. Many youths have

> **"You care so much about being accepted by other kids,"** said Debbie. **"I dreaded the thought of being unpopular . . . I feared I would be isolated"**

viewpoints and opinions that are unsound, unreliable, even reckless. So when a youth unquestioningly comes under the control of peers, it may be little more than the blind leading the blind. (Compare Matthew 15:14.) The results can be disastrous.

Even when peers are not edging you toward outrageous behavior, their influence can still feel oppressive. "You care so much about being accepted by other kids," said Debbie. "When I was eighteen I dreaded the thought of being unpopular because I would have no one to invite me out for a good time. I feared I would be isolated." Debbie thus worked hard to gain the acceptance of her peers.

Am I Being Influenced?

Have you too begun to dress, talk, or act a certain way in order to fit in? Seventeen-year-old Susie claims, "Another kid can't really make you do anything you don't want to do." True, but peer pressure can be so subtle that you may not realize how much it is affecting you. Consider, for example, the apostle Peter. A bold man with strong conviction, Peter was a pillar of Christianity. God revealed to Peter that people from all nations and races could gain His favor. Peter thus helped the first Gentile believers to become Christians.—Acts 10:28.

However, time passed, and Peter was situated in Antioch, a city in which many non-Jews had become

'*I Dare You!*'

"Go on," insisted Lisa's classmates. "Tell the teacher her breath stinks!" No, oral hygiene was hardly the issue. Lisa was being challenged to take a dare—and a rather risky one at that! Yes, some youths seem to get perverse pleasure out of challenging others to perform acts that range from mildly mischievous to simply suicidal.

But when you are challenged to do something silly, unkind, or downright dangerous, it's time to think twice. Said a wise man: "Dead flies are what cause the oil of the ointment maker to stink, to bubble forth. So a little foolishness does to one who is precious for wisdom and glory." (Ecclesiastes 10:1) In ancient times, a valuable ointment or perfume could be ruined by something as tiny as a dead fly. Similarly, one's hard-earned reputation could be ruined by just "a little foolishness."

Childish pranks often result in lower grades, suspension from school, and even arrest! What, though, if you think you won't get caught? Ask yourself, Is what I am being asked to do reasonable? Is it loving? Will it violate the standards of the Bible or those taught by my parents? If so, do I really want fun-seeking youths to control my life? Are youths who ask me to put my life and reputation on the line really friends, anyway?—Proverbs 18:24.

Try, then, to reason with the youth making the dare. Eighteen-year-old Terry likes to "take the fun out of it" by asking, 'Why should I do it? What would it prove if I did it?' Also let it be known that you have definite standards you intend to live by. One young girl tried to dare a boy into immorality, saying, "You don't know what you're missing." "Yes, I do," the boy replied. "Herpes, gonorrhea, syphilis . . . "

Yes, by having the courage to say no to your peers, you can avoid doing something you would later regret!

Christians. Peter freely socialized with these Gentile believers. One day some Jewish Christians from Jerusalem, still harboring prejudices against non-Jews, visited Antioch. How would Peter now conduct himself around his Jewish peers?

Well, Peter separated himself from the Gentile Christians, refusing to eat with them! Why? He apparently feared offending his peers. He may have reasoned, 'I'll just bend a little now while they're here and continue eating with the Gentiles after they've gone. Why ruin my rapport with them over such a small thing?' Peter was thus putting on a pretense—rejecting his own principles by doing something he really did not believe in. (Galatians 2:11-14) Obviously, then, no one is immune to pressure from peers.

Youths often cling to one another for support

Have you ever been pressured by peers to go against what you know is right?

How Would I React?

So while it is easy to say, 'I'm not afraid of what others think!' maintaining that resolve in the face of peer pressure is quite another thing. For example, what would you do in the following circumstances?

One of your schoolmates offers you a cigarette in front of other youths. You know it is wrong to smoke. But they are all waiting to see what you will do . . .

The girls in school are talking about having sex with their boyfriends. One of the girls says to you: "You're not still a virgin, are you?"

You wanted to wear a dress like the one all the other girls are wearing, but Mom says it's too short. The outfit she insists on your wearing makes you feel like you look six years old. Your classmates tease you. One girl asks, "Why don't you just save up your lunch money and buy something decent? You don't have to let your mother know. Just keep your school clothes in your locker."

Easy situations to face? No, but if you are afraid to say no to your peers, you end up saying no to yourself, to your standards, and to your parents. How can you develop the strength to stand up to peer pressure?

"Thinking Ability"

Fifteen-year-old Robin started smoking, not because she wanted to, but because everyone else did. She recalls: "Later on I began to think, 'I don't like it. Why am I doing it?' So I don't anymore." By thinking for herself, she was able to stand up to her peers!

Appropriately, then, the Bible urges youths to develop "knowledge and thinking ability." (Proverbs 1:1-5) One with thinking ability does not have to lean upon inexperienced peers for direction. At the same time, that one does not become self-confident and ignore the opinions of others. (Proverbs 14:16) He or she is willing to "listen to counsel and accept discipline" so as to "become wise."—Proverbs 19:20.

Don't be surprised, though, if you are disliked or even ridiculed for using your thinking faculties. "The man [or woman] of thinking abilities is hated," says Proverbs 14:17. But really, who has more strength, those who give in to their passions and emotions or those who can say no to improper desires? (Compare Proverbs 16:32.) Where are those who ridicule you headed in life? Is that where you want your life to end up also? Could it be that

Have the strength to stand up to peer pressure!

such ones are simply jealous of you and are covering up their own insecurity by ridicule?

Escaping the Snare

"Trembling at men is what lays a snare," says Proverbs 29:25. In Bible times, a snare could quickly trap any unsuspecting animal that grabbed its bait. Today, the desire to be accepted by your peers can likewise serve as bait. It can lure you into the trap of violating godly standards. How, then, can you escape—or avoid—the snare of the fear of man?

First, choose your friends carefully! (Proverbs 13: 20) Associate with those who have Christian values and standards. True, this limits your friendships. As one teenager says: "When I didn't go along with others in school, with their ideas on drugs and sex, they soon left me alone. Although this lifted a lot of pressure off me to conform, it did make me feel a little lonesome." But it is better to suffer some loneliness than to let peer influence drag you down spiritually and morally. Association within one's family and within the Christian congregation can help fill the vacuum of loneliness.

Listening to your parents also helps you resist peer pressure. (Proverbs 23:22) They are likely working hard to teach you proper values. One young girl said: "My parents were firm with me. I didn't like it at times, but I'm glad they put their foot down and limited my associations." Because of that parental help, she did not give in to pressure to use drugs and engage in sex.

Teen adviser Beth Winship further observes: "Adolescents who are good at something feel important in their own right. They don't have to depend on peer approval for good self-image." Why not, then, strive to be skillful and competent in what you do at school and around the house? Young witnesses of Jehovah particularly strive to be 'workmen with nothing to be ashamed of, handling the word of the truth aright' in their Christian ministry. — 2 Timothy 2:15.

After warning about the "snare" of fearing men, Proverbs 29:25 continues: "He that is trusting in Jehovah will be protected." Perhaps more than anything else, a relationship with God can strengthen you to stand up to your peers. For example, Debbie (mentioned earlier) had been a follower of the crowd for some time, drinking heavily and abusing drugs. But then she began a serious study of the Bible and began to trust in Jehovah. The effect? "I made up my mind that I wasn't going to do the same things as that little group of kids," said Debbie. She told her former friends: "You go your way and I'll go mine. If you want my friendship you will have to respect the same standards I do. I'm sorry but I just don't care what you think. This is what I'm going to do." Not all of Debbie's friends respected her newfound faith. But says Debbie, "I sure liked myself better after I made my decision."

You too will 'like yourself better' and spare yourself much grief if you escape the trap of peer pressure!

Questions for Discussion   Chapter 9

☐ *Why are youths inclined to be influenced by their peers? Is this necessarily bad?*

☐ *What does the experience of the apostle Peter teach regarding peer pressure?*

☐ *What are some situations (including perhaps some from personal experience) that might test your ability to say no?*

☐ *What things might you consider if challenged to take a dare?*

☐ *What are some things that can help you escape the snare of fear of man?*

A Look at How You Look

They say that beauty is only skin-deep. Why is it, though, that the good-looking youths seem to get all the advantages? And how is a youth to cope with all the pressure to dress and look like his or her peers?

The next few pages are designed to help you take a fresh and realistic look at that face you see in the mirror each morning.

Chapter 10

How Important Are Looks?

YOU say you don't like the way you look? Well, few of us—if any—are entirely satisfied with our appearance. Unlike Narcissus, who fell in love with his reflection in a pool of water, some of us nearly fall into depression when we see our reflection.

'I've got this dislike about my body,' laments 16-year-old Maria. 'I think I don't look so good.' Thirteen-year-old Bob has a similar grievance: 'I don't like my hair, the way it sticks up here in the back.' To make matters worse, a teenager's appearance can change so rapidly that, according to one psychologist, youths often "feel like strangers in their own bodies." Many thus fret about their face, hair, figure, and physique.

'I've got this dislike about my body . . . I think I don't look so good'

Of course, God himself has an appreciation for beauty. Says Ecclesiastes 3:11: "Everything [God] has made pretty in its time." And how you look can indeed have a profound effect upon the way others view and treat you. Adds Dr. James P. Comer: "Body image is part of self-image. It can affect a person's self-confidence and what he does and does not do in life." A healthy concern about your appearance thus makes good sense. However, when you become so self-conscious that you withdraw from others or feel bad about yourself, then such concern is no longer healthy.

What you dislike about yourself may be envied by others

Who Says You're Unattractive?

Interestingly, distress over personal appearance is not always due to real physical defects. A slender girl sits in class wishing she was heavier, while on the next aisle, a buxom girl laments how "fat" she is. From where does such dissatisfaction come? What makes well-formed youths think they are unattractive?

Says professor of psychiatry Richard M. Sarles: "Adolescence is a period of transition in which a major reorganization of the body takes place. . . . To deal with the awkwardness of a new and changing body, most adolescents rely upon the security of their peer group." But under the scrutiny of your peers, how tall, short, fat, or thin you are—not to mention the shape of your nose or ears—can become a source of great anxiety. And when others get more attention than you or when you are chided about your looks, you can easily begin to feel bad about yourself.

Then there is the pervasive influence of TV, books, and movies. Attractive men and women stare at us from TV screens and magazine pages, selling everything from perfume to chain saws. The communications

'Can't I Do Something About My Acne?'

Acne is a disorder of the skin that causes it to be spotted or even disfigured by pimples, blackheads, red swellings, or cysts. For many youths, it is a serious skin disorder, rather than merely a passing discomfort that lasts only a few months. People of all ages can be afflicted with it, but teenagers suffer the most. According to some experts, about 80 percent develop acne in varying degrees.

Not surprisingly, when 2,000 teenagers were asked to say what they disliked most about themselves, problems with skin far outnumbered every other complaint. Recalls a youth named Sandra, who had a bad case of acne while still in high school: "I had such bad acne, I was always hiding my face from other people. I was shy because I was embarrassed about the way I looked. . . . I looked so bad."—Co-Ed magazine.

Why does this scourge appear during your teen years —at the very time you want to look your best? Because you are growing up. With the onset of puberty, skin glands increase their activity.

What happens? The World Book Encyclopedia explains in simple terms: Each gland empties into a hair follicle —that is, the little bag surrounding each hair. Normally, the oil would drain out through a pore of the skin, but sometimes a pore gets clogged and the oil cannot get out quickly enough. The clogged pore now forms a blemish called a blackhead because the trapped oil oxidizes, dries, and turns black. A pimple develops when pus forms. Cysts are formed when germs breed in the backed-up oil. It is the cysts that leave permanent scars. Pimples do not scar unless they become infected, which often happens as a result of squeezing or picking —so don't squeeze or pick!

Interestingly, tension and emotional upsets can activate the skin glands. Some experience the blossoming of a large pimple just before an important event or before and during exams. Jesus' words are thus practical: "Never be anxious about the next day, for the next day will have its own anxieties."—Matthew 6:34.

Sad to say, no miracle cure exists. There are, however, over-the-counter medications available, such as gels, creams, lotions, washes, soaps, and facial masks, containing benzoyl peroxide (an antibacterial agent) that can help bring acne under control. (Your family doctor can be consulted if stronger measures are needed.) Many find that cleansing their skin thoroughly with a soap or wash containing benzoyl peroxide is helpful. However, avoid oily soaps or oil-based cosmetics.

Some youths have also found that by taking care of their overall health—getting plenty of exercise, being out in the fresh air as much as possible, and getting enough sleep—their acne condition improves. And while the benefits of maintaining a fat-free diet are debated by some, avoiding junk food, as well as eating a balanced diet, obviously makes sense.

HOW IMPORTANT ARE LOOKS?

In any event, patience is a must. Remember: The problem built up over quite a period of time, so it will not clear up overnight. Sandra, mentioned earlier, says: "I guess it took about a year for my skin to completely clear up, but I could see changes in my skin within six weeks." By sticking to your treatment over a period of time, you may experience some relief.

Meanwhile, do not let a few blemishes crush your self-esteem or inhibit your talking with others. While you may feel quite self-conscious about your skin, others probably notice it a lot less than you think. So try to keep a positive, happy spirit. And do what you can for your acne right now!

media would thus have you believe that if you're not a flawless-skinned beauty or a muscular "hunk," you might as well crawl into a hole somewhere—or at least forget about ever being popular or happy.

Don't Be 'Squeezed Into Their Mold'!

But before concluding that you are an ugly duckling, ask yourself to what extent your physical flaws are real —or imagined. Is that facial feature you fret (or are teased) about really so unattractive? Or have others pressured you into thinking it is? The Bible advises: "Don't let the world around you squeeze you into its own mould."—Romans 12:2, *Phillips.*

Think: Who is it that promotes the idea that you need a certain look if you are to be popular, successful, or happy? Is it not manufacturers and advertisers who stand to profit by your pursuing fad diets or purchasing expensive beauty aids? Why let them mold your thinking? And if peers are critical of your looks, are they doing so to be helpful—or simply to put you down? If the latter is true, who needs "friends" like that, anyway?

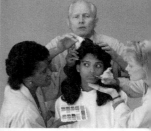

Youths often fail to appreciate that magazine models have the services of a beauty-support team

talks about the way people looked? Why aren't we told what Abraham, Mary, or even Jesus looked like? Obviously, God did not consider it important.

Interestingly, God once rejected for the position of king a young man named Eliab, whose stature was most impressive! Jehovah God explained to the prophet Samuel: "Do not look at his appearance and at the height of his stature . . . For not the way man sees is the way God sees, because mere man sees what appears to the eyes; but as for Jehovah, he sees what the heart is." (1 Samuel 16:6, 7) What a comfort it is to know that to God, the One who really counts, our looks are not the important thing! "He sees what the heart is."

Another point to ponder: Are not most of your friends rather average-looking? And would either of your parents be material for the cover of a fashion magazine? Probably not. Indeed, knowing their fine qualities, you seldom even think about their looks! You too have assets as a person that far outweigh any physical deficiencies—real or imagined.

Nevertheless, looks are important to your peers, and you may find yourself under pressure to conform to their styles of dress and grooming. How should you respond to that pressure?

Questions for Discussion	*Chapter 10*

☐ *Why are youths so concerned about their looks? How do you feel about your own looks?*

☐ *What view of the importance of looks is promoted by the media and your peers? How should you respond to such influence?*

☐ *What are some ways of dealing with the problem of acne?*

☐ *How can you make the most of your looks? Why is there a need for balance in this regard?*

Chapter 11

Do My Clothes Reveal the Real Me?

"IT'S *not* too short," Peggy cried to her parents. "You're just being old-fashioned!" Off she ran to her room—the grand finale to a quarrel over a skirt she wanted to wear. And perhaps you have been the center of a similar controversy when a parent, a teacher, or an employer criticized some outfit that you loved. You called it casual; they called it sloppy. You called it chic; they called it gaudy or suggestive.

Admittedly, tastes vary, and you do have a right to your opinions. But should this mean that 'anything goes' when it comes to how you dress?

The Right Message?

"What you wear," says a girl named Pam, "is really who you are and how you feel about yourself." Yes, clothing sends out a message, a statement to others about *you.* Clothing can whisper conscientiousness, stability, high moral standards. Or it can shout rebellion and discontent. It can even serve as a form of identification. Some youths use ripped clothing, punk styles, or expensive designer clothes as a type of trademark. Others use clothing to attract the opposite sex or to make themselves appear older than they really are.

It is thus easy to see why clothing is so important to many youths. However, John T. Molloy, author of *Dress for Success,* cautions: "The way we dress has a remarkable impact on the people we meet and greatly affects how they treat us."

YOUNG PEOPLE ASK . . .

Parents often clash with their children over what they wear. Are the parents simply being old-fashioned?

No wonder your parents are so concerned about how you dress! To them it is more than an issue of personal taste. They want you to send out the right message, one that projects you as a balanced, responsible person. Does the way you dress, however, accomplish this? What guides your selection of clothes?

"I Do Whatever My Friends Want to Do"

For many youths, clothing is a statement of their independence and individuality. But as a youth, your personality is still in a state of flux—still developing, still changing. So while you want to make a statement concerning yourself, you may not be too sure what that statement should say or how to say it. Some youths thus adorn themselves in bizarre, outrageous attire. Instead of establishing their 'individuality,' however, they are merely calling attention to their immaturity—not to mention embarrassing their parents.

Other youths simply choose to dress like their peers; it seems to give them a sense of security and identity with a group. Of course, it's not necessarily wrong to want to blend in with people. (Compare 1 Corinthians 9:22.) But would a Christian really want to be identified with unbelieving youths? And is it wise to seek peer approval at any cost? One young girl confessed: "I do whatever my friends want to do just so they won't say something." But what do you call someone who is at the beck and call of someone else, who gives in to someone else's whim and fancy? The Bible answers: "Do you not know that if you keep presenting yourselves to anyone . . . to obey him, you are *slaves* of him because you obey him?"—Romans 6:16.

Among young people "the emphasis on compliance can become so strong that group members almost seem to be prisoners of group norms, depending on them [their peers] for advice on how to dress, how to talk, what to do, and even what to think and believe."—*Adolescence: Transition From Childhood to Maturity*.

But how qualified are your friends to give such advice? (Compare Matthew 15:14.) Are they not suffering the same emotional growing pains that you are? Is it wise, then, meekly to let them set your standards—even when such go against your common sense or the values and the wishes of your parents?

"In" Today—"Out" Tomorrow

Other youths are guided by the winds of fashion. But how temperamental those winds are! We are reminded of the Bible's words: "The scene of this world is changing." (1 Corinthians 7:31) What is "in" today can thus become obsolete tomorrow with astonishing (not to mention expensive) suddenness. Hemlines rise and fall, trouser legs flare and taper, all to the benefit of manufacturers and clothing designers who reap rich profits from an easily manipulated public.

Consider, for example, the designer-jean fad of a few years

*M*any youths try to assert their individuality through outlandish attire

Dress in a manner appropriate to the circumstances. Clothing sends out a message about you!

back. Jeans suddenly became high fashion. People paid extravagant prices to be walking billboards bearing such names as Calvin Klein and Gloria Vanderbilt. "People want a name," explained Eli Kaplan, president of the company manufacturing "Sergio Valente" jeans. Who, though, is this Mr. Valente, whose prestigious name is so conspicuously sewn on jeans' pockets? "He doesn't exist," reported *Newsweek*. And in explanation Kaplan himself asked: "Who was going to buy Eli Kaplan jeans?"

'But is it wrong to be in style?' you might ask. Not necessarily. Servants of God in Bible times attired themselves according to local tastes. For example, the Bible says that Tamar wore a striped robe, "for that was the way the daughters of the king, the virgins, used to dress" in those days. —2 Samuel 13:18.

But should one be enslaved to style? One young girl lamented: "You see in a store a great pair of pants that everybody else has and you say, 'Mom, get me those pants,' and she

DO MY CLOTHES REVEAL THE REAL ME?

says, 'No, I can make them at home.' I say, 'But you don't understand. I want *these* pants.'" Really, though, doesn't your being a pawn of fashion designers strip you of your individuality and obscure the real you? Why should you be controlled by provocative ads, slogans, and designer names?

> "*What you wear is really who you are and how you feel about yourself*"

The Bible tells us at Romans 12:2: "Quit being fashioned after this system of things, but be transformed by making your mind over, that you may prove to yourselves the good and acceptable and perfect will of God." What is the 'acceptable will of God' when it comes to your choice of clothing?

'Modest and Well Arranged'

First Timothy 2:9 encourages Christians to "adorn themselves in well-arranged dress, with modesty and soundness of mind." "Well-arranged dress" would naturally be neat and clean. "Modesty" takes circumstances into consideration. A well-tailored suit may be appropriate for a job, but it is out of place at the beach! Conversely, a swimsuit would be considered ludicrous in an office.

Young witnesses of Jehovah would thus be concerned that what they wear at Christian meetings or in the work of preaching to others is not overly casual but identifies them as young ministers of God. Recall Paul's words at 2 Corinthians 6:3, 4: "In no way are we giving any cause for stumbling, that our ministry might not be found fault with; but in every way we recommend ourselves as God's ministers."

Modesty also takes into consideration the feelings of others. As the apostle Paul put it, a Christian's actions should take into account not only his own conscience "but that of the other person." (1 Corinthians 10:29) Should you not be particularly concerned with the conscience of your parents?

The Benefits of Dressing Appropriately

The Bible tells of a time when Queen Esther needed to appear before her husband, the king. However, such an unbidden appearance could be a capital offense! No doubt Esther fervently prayed for God's help. But she also paid attention to her appearance by "dressing up royally"—in a manner suitable for the occasion! And "as soon as the king saw Esther the queen standing in the courtyard, she gained favor in his eyes."—Esther 5:1, 2.

Your being dressed in an attractive but modest manner might help you to make a good impression at a job interview. Vicki L. Baum, director of a Career Development Center, observes: "Some women get confused when they go for an interview. They think it's like going on a date, and they look seductive." The results? "It takes away from your professionalism." She advises against wearing "things that are tight or suggestive."

Young men, too, should strive to wear well-arranged clothing when job hunting. John T. Molloy notes that businessmen "have their hair combed and their shoes shined. And they expect the same of other men."

Immodest attire, though, can damage your relationships with others. *Psychology Today* referred to a survey taken among adolescents that showed that "a lowcut top, shorts, tight jeans, or no bra" would likely be interpreted by males as a sexual come-on. One young man confessed: "I personally find it rather hard to think only pure thoughts about younger women when I see the way they dress." Modest attire allows people to appreciate your *inner qualities.* If you're not sure a certain outfit is modest, ask your parents for advice.

Dressing Up "the Inner Man"

The apostle Peter encouraged Christians to let their adornment be "the secret person of the heart in the incorruptible apparel of the quiet and mild spirit, which is of great value in the eyes of God"—yes, and in the eyes of others! (1 Peter 3:4) Fashionable dress may dazzle some of your peers. But clothes do not win hearts or make real friends. This is accomplished by dressing up "the inner man"—working on the person you are inside. (2 Corinthians 4:16, *The Jerusalem Bible*) A person who is inwardly beautiful will always be attractive to others, even if his or her clothes are not the latest style or "tattooed" with silly designer labels.

Who knows what fad will next send youths stampeding into the stores. You, however, can think for yourself. Hold to high standards of dress. Avoid faddish attire and clothes that stress sexuality. Be on the conservative side, not being the first—nor necessarily the last—to jump on the fashion bandwagon. Look for quality garments that will last—not quickly drop out of fashion. Be sure that your clothes send out the right message, displaying, not some image conjured up by the media or peers, but the *real you!*

Questions for Discussion   *Chapter 11*

□ *How does clothing send out a message?*

□ *Why do some youths lean toward the bizarre in their choice of clothes?*

□ *How much are you influenced by your peers when it comes to choice of clothing?*

□ *What are some disadvantages of always trying to be in style?*

□ *What determines if a style is 'modest and well arranged'?*

Why Do I Feel This Way?

Lonely, depressed, sullen, discouraged—is this the way you feel most of the time? Of course not! Like most youths you probably feel rather good about yourself. Nevertheless, from time to time even the best of us get a dose of negative emotions. Read on and find out how you can better understand yourself and deal with such feelings.

Chapter 12

Why Don't I Like Myself?

"I DON'T feel very special at all," lamented Louise. Do you, too, occasionally feel bad about yourself?

Really, everyone needs a certain amount of self-esteem. It has been called "the ingredient that gives dignity to human existence." Further, the Bible says: "You must love your neighbor *as yourself*." (Matthew 19:19) And if you feel bad about yourself, you will probably feel bad about others too.

'I Can't Do Anything Right!'

Why might you have these negative feelings about yourself? For one thing, your limitations may frustrate you. You are growing up, and often there is a period of awkwardness in which dropping things or bumping into them is a daily embarrassment. Then, too, you simply don't have an adult's experience in bouncing back from disappointments. And because your "perceptive powers" haven't been sufficiently trained "through use," you may not always make the wisest decisions. (Hebrews 5:14) At times you may feel that you can't do anything right!

Self-esteem has been called "the ingredient that gives dignity to human existence"

Failure to meet one's parents' expectations can be another cause of low self-esteem. "If I make an 'A minus' in school," one youth says, "my folks want to

Do you feel dejected, inferior? There is a solution

know why it wasn't an 'A' and tell me I'm a failure." Of course, it's instinctive for parents to urge their children to do their very best. And when you fall short of reasonable expectations, you can be sure that you will hear about it. The Bible's counsel is: "Listen, my son [or daughter], to the discipline of your father, and do not forsake the law of your mother." (Proverbs 1:8, 9) Instead of feeling discouraged, take criticism in stride and learn from it.

What, though, if one's folks make unfair comparisons? ("Why can't you be like your older brother, Paul? He was always an honor student.") Such comparisons, hurtful though they may seem at the time, often make a valid point. Your folks just want the best for you. And if you feel they're being too hard on you, why not discuss matters with them calmly?

Building Self-Respect

How can you bolster sagging self-esteem? First, take an honest look at your assets and liabilities. You will discover that many of your so-called liabilities are quite petty. What about serious flaws, such as a quick temper or selfishness? Conscientiously work on these problems and your self-respect is sure to grow.

Furthermore, do not blind yourself to the fact that

you already have assets! You may not think that being able to cook or to fix a flat tire is that important. But a hungry person or a stranded motorist will admire you for having such skills! Think, too, of your virtues. Are you studious? Patient? Compassionate? Generous? Kind? These qualities far outweigh minor flaws.

It may also help to consider this brief checklist:

Set realistic goals: If you always shoot for the stars, you can suffer bitter disappointment. Set goals that are attainable. How about learning a skill such as typing? Learn to play a musical instrument or to speak another language. Improve or branch out in your reading. Self-respect is a useful by-product of accomplishment.

Do good work: If you do shoddy work, you're not going to feel good about yourself. God took pleasure in his creative works and declared the creative epochs to be "good" at their completion. (Genesis 1:3-31) You, too, can take pleasure in whatever work you do at home or in school by doing it skillfully and conscientiously. —See Proverbs 22:29.

Do things for others: Self-respect is not gained by sitting back and letting others wait on you hand and foot. Jesus said that "whoever wants to become great . . . must be [a] minister," or servant, for others. —Mark 10:43-45.

For example, 17-year-old Kim budgeted 60 hours each month of summer vacation to help others learn Bible truths. She says: "It has brought me closer to Jehovah. It has also helped me to develop a real love for people." It is not likely that this happy young woman will be lacking in self-respect!

Pick your friends carefully: "My relationship with myself is a very unhappy one," said 17-year-old Barbara. "When I am with people who have confidence in me, I do good work. With those who treat me as an accessory to a machine, I become stupid."

People who are high-minded or insulting can indeed make you feel bad about yourself. So pick friends who are truly interested in your welfare, friends who build you up.—Proverbs 13:20.

Make God your closest friend: "Jehovah is my crag and my stronghold," declared the psalmist David. (Psalm 18:2) His confidence was not in his own abilities but in his close friendship with Jehovah. Thus, when adversity later struck him, he could withstand severe criticism without losing his composure. (2 Samuel 16: 7, 10) You, too, can "draw close to God" and thus "boast," not in yourself, but in Jehovah!—James 2:21-23; 4:8; 1 Corinthians 1:31.

Dead Ends

One writer said: "Sometimes the adolescent with a weak identity and low self-esteem tries to develop a false front or facade with which to face the world." The roles some assume are familiar: The "tough guy," the promiscuous socialite, the outrageously clad punk rocker. But beneath the facades, such youths still grapple with feelings of inferiority.—Proverbs 14:13.

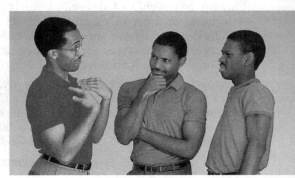

Becoming a boaster or a braggart is no solution to having low self-esteem

Do you sometimes feel you can't do anything right?

Consider, for example, those who indulge in promiscuity "to banish feelings of depression, to increase self-esteem [by feeling wanted], to achieve intimacy and, with pregnancy, to gain the love and unquestioning acceptance of another human being—a baby." (*Coping With Teenage Depression*) One disenchanted young woman wrote: "I tried to substitute sexual intimacy as a comfort, rather than trying to build a solid relationship with my Creator. All I built was emptiness, loneliness and more depression." Beware, then, of such dead ends.

A Word of Caution

Interestingly, the Scriptures frequently warn against thinking *too highly* of oneself! Why is this? Apparently because most of us, in our efforts to gain self-confidence, tend to overshoot the mark. Many become egotistical and grossly exaggerate their skills and abilities. Some elevate themselves by putting others down.

Back in the first century, intense rivalry between Jews and Gentiles (non-Jews) afflicted a Christian congregation in Rome. So the apostle Paul reminded the Gentiles that only by means of God's "kindness" had they been "grafted" into a position of God's favor. (Romans 11:17-36) Self-righteous Jews, too, had to confront their imperfections. "For all have sinned and fall short of the glory of God," said Paul.—Romans 3:23.

Paul did not strip them of self-esteem but said: "For through the undeserved kindness given to me I tell everyone . . . not to think more of himself than it is necessary to think." (Romans 12:3) So while it is "necessary" to have a measure of self-respect, one should not go to extremes in this regard.

As Dr. Allan Fromme observes: "A person who has an adequate conception of himself is not sad, but he does not have to be deliriously happy. . . . He is not pessimistic, but his optimism is not unbridled. He is neither foolhardy nor free of specific fears . . . He realizes that he is not the outstanding success of all time, nor is he a perennial [continual] failure."

So be modest. "God opposes the haughty ones, but he gives undeserved kindness to the humble ones." (James 4:6) Acknowledge your assets, but don't ignore your faults. Rather, work on them. You'll still doubt yourself from time to time. But you need not ever doubt your self-worth or that God cares for you. For "if anyone loves God, this one is known by him."—1 Corinthians 8:3.

Questions for Discussion   *Chapter 12*

☐ *Why do some youths have negative feelings about themselves? Can you relate to the way such youths feel?*

☐ *How might you handle the demands of your parents?*

☐ *What are some ways to build self-respect?*

☐ *What are some dead ends to building self-esteem?*

☐ *Why must you be careful not to think too highly of yourself?*

Chapter 13

Why Do I Get So Depressed?

Melanie had always lived up to her mother's ideal of the perfect child—until she turned 17. Then she withdrew from school activities, stopped accepting invitations to parties, and didn't even seem to care when her grades dropped from A's to C's. When her parents gently inquired what was wrong, she stormed away saying, "Leave me alone! There's nothing wrong."

Mark, at 14, was impulsive and hostile, with an explosive temper. At school he was fidgety and disruptive. When frustrated or angry, he would race across the desert on a motorcycle or shoot down steep hills on his skateboard.

MELANIE and Mark both suffered forms of the same malady—depression. Dr. Donald McKnew of the National Institute of Mental Health says that 10 to 15 percent of schoolchildren may suffer mood disorders. A smaller number suffer from severe depression.

At times there is a biologic basis for the problem. Some infections or endocrine-system diseases, the hormonal shifts of the menstrual cycle, hypoglycemia, certain medications, exposure to toxic metals or chemicals, allergic reactions, an unbalanced diet, anemia—all of these can trigger depression.

Pressures at the Root of Depression

However, the teen years themselves are often the source of emotional stress. Not having an adult's experience in handling life's ups and downs, a youth can feel that no one cares and could become painfully depressed over relatively commonplace matters.

Failing to measure up to the expectations of parents, teachers, or friends is another cause of melancholy. Donald, for example, felt that he had to excel in school to please his well-educated parents. Failing to do that, he became depressed and suicidal. "I have never done anything right. I have always let everybody down," lamented Donald.

That a sense of failure can kindle depression is evident from the case of a man named Epaphroditus. During the first century, this faithful Christian was sent on a special mission to assist the imprisoned apostle Paul. But when he reached Paul he soon fell sick—and Paul, instead, had to care for him! You can imagine, then, why Epaphroditus might have felt like such a failure and became "depressed." Apparently he overlooked all the good he had performed before he got sick.—Philippians 2:25-30.

A Sense of Loss

Francine Klagsbrun wrote in her book *Too Young to Die—Youth and Suicide:* "At the root of many emotionally caused depressions lies a profound sense of loss, of someone or something that has been deeply loved." Thus the loss of a parent through death or divorce, the loss of a job or career, or even the loss of one's physical health could also be at the root of depression.

A most devastating loss to a young person, though, is the loss of love, the feeling of being unwanted and uncared for. "When my mother left us I felt betrayed and alone," revealed a young woman named Marie. "My world suddenly seemed upside down."

Imagine, then, the bewilderment and pain some youths feel when faced with family problems such as divorce, alcoholism, incest, wife beating, child abuse, or simple rejection by a parent who is swallowed up in his or her own problems. How true the Bible proverb: "Have you shown yourself discouraged in the day of distress? Your power [including the ability to resist depression] will be scanty"! (Proverbs 24:10) A youth may even mistakenly blame himself for his family's problems.

Recognizing the Symptoms

There are different degrees of depression. A young person might temporarily be demoralized by some up-setting event. But usually such blues fade in a relatively short time.

Severe depression is the most common factor in teen suicides

However, if the depressed mood lingers and the youth has a general negative feeling along with feelings of worthlessness, anxiety, and anger, this can develop into what doctors call low-grade chronic depression. As the experiences of Mark and Melanie (mentioned at the outset) show, the symptoms can vary considerably. One young person may have anxiety attacks. Another may be tired all the time, have no appetite, experience trouble in sleeping, lose weight, or suffer a series of accidents.

Some young persons try to hide depression by embarking upon a pleasure binge: an endless round of parties, sexual promiscuity, vandalism, heavy drinking,

*C*ould It Be Major Depression?

Anyone may suffer temporarily from one or more of the following symptoms without having a serious problem. However, if several symptoms persist, or if any is severe enough that it interferes with your normal activities, you may have (1) a physical illness and need a thorough examination by a doctor or (2) a serious mental disorder —major depression.

Nothing Gives You Pleasure. You can't find pleasure in activities you once enjoyed. You feel unreal, as if in a fog and just going through the motions of living.

Total Worthlessness. You feel that your life has nothing important to contribute and is totally useless. You may feel full of guilt.

Drastic Change of Mood. If you were once outgoing, you may become withdrawn or vice versa. You may often cry.

Total Hopelessness. You feel that things are bad, there's nothing you can do about them, and conditions will never get better.

Wish You Were Dead. The anguish is so great that you frequently feel that you would be better off dead.

Cannot Concentrate. You go over and over certain thoughts or you read without comprehension.

Change in Eating or Bowel Habits. Loss of appetite or overeating. Intermittent constipation or diarrhea.

Sleeping Habits Change. Poor or excessive sleep. You may frequently have nightmares.

Aches and Pains. Headaches, cramps, and pains in the abdomen and chest. You may constantly feel tired for no good reason.

Failure to live up to one's parents' expectations can cause a youth to feel depressed

and the like. "I don't really know why I have to be going out all the time," confessed one 14-year-old boy. "I just know if I'm by myself, alone, I realize how bad I feel." It is just as the Bible described: "Even in laughter the heart may be in pain."—Proverbs 14:13.

When It's More Than Just the Blues

If low-grade chronic depression is not dealt with, it can progress to a more serious disorder—major depression. (See page 107.) "I constantly felt as if I were 'dead' inside," explained Marie, a victim of major depression. "I was just existing without any emotions. I had a feeling of constant dread." In major depression the gloomy mood is unrelenting and may continue for months. Consequently, this type of depression is the most common ingredient in teen suicides—now considered a "hidden epidemic" in many countries.

The most persistent emotion connected with major depression—and the deadliest—is a deep sense of hopelessness. Professor John E. Mack writes of a 14-year-old named Vivienne, who was a victim of major depression. To all outward appearances she was a perfect young lady with caring parents. Yet, in the depths of despair, she hanged herself! Wrote Professor Mack:

"Vivienne's inability to foresee that her depression would ever lift, that she had any hope of ultimately obtaining relief from her pain, is an important element in her decision to kill herself."

Those affected with major depression thus feel as if they will never get better, that there is no tomorrow. Such hopelessness, according to experts, often leads to suicidal behavior.

Suicide, however, is not the answer. Marie, whose life had become a living nightmare, confessed: "The thoughts of suicide definitely came into my mind. But I realized that as long as I didn't kill myself there was always hope." Ending it all indeed solves nothing. Unfortunately, when confronted with despair, many young persons cannot even visualize alternatives or the possibility of a favorable outcome. Marie thus tried to hide her problem by injecting herself with heroin. She said: "I had plenty of self-confidence—until the drug wore off."

Dealing With Minor Distress

There are sensible ways of dealing with feelings of depression. "Some people get depressed because they're hungry," observed Dr. Nathan S. Kline, a New

Talking to others and pouring out your heart is one of the best ways to cope

Doing things for others is yet another way to beat the blues

York specialist on depression. "A person may not eat breakfast and for some reason miss lunch. Then by three o'clock he begins wondering why he doesn't feel right."

What you eat can also make a difference. Debbie, a young woman plagued with feelings of despair, admitted: "I didn't realize that junk food was so detrimental to my mood. I ate a lot of it. Now I notice that when I eat fewer sweets, I feel better." Other helpful steps: Some form of exercise may lift your spirits. In some cases, a medical checkup would be in order, since depression can be a symptom of physical illness.

Winning the Battle of the Mind

Often depression is brought on or made worse by having negative thoughts about yourself. "When you've been through a lot of people cutting at you," lamented 18-year-old Evelyn, "it makes you think you're not worth anything."

Consider: Is it up to others to measure your worth as a person? Similar ridicule was heaped upon the Christian apostle Paul. Some said that he was a weakling and a poor speaker. Did this make Paul feel worthless? Not at all! Paul knew that meeting God's standard was the important thing. He could boast over what he had accomplished with God's help—regardless of what others were saying. If you, too, remind yourself of the fact that you have a standing with God, the gloomy mood will often leave.—2 Corinthians 10:7, 10, 17, 18.

What if you are depressed because of some weakness or sin you have committed? "Though the sins of you people should prove to be as scarlet," God told Israel, "they will be made white just like snow." (Isaiah 1:18) Never overlook the compassion and patience of our heavenly Father. (Psalm 103:8-14) But are you also striving hard to overcome your problem? You must do your part if you are to ease your mind of feelings of guilt. As the proverb says: "He that is confessing and leaving [his transgressions] will be shown mercy." —Proverbs 28:13.

Another way to fight the blues is to set realistic goals for yourself. You don't have to be top in your school class to be successful. (Ecclesiastes 7:16-18) Accept the fact that disappointments are a part of life. When these occur, rather than feel, 'No one cares what happens to me and no one ever will,' tell yourself, 'I'll get over it.' And there's nothing wrong with having a good cry.

The Value of Accomplishment

"Despair doesn't go away on its own," advises Daphne, who successfully lived through bouts of discouragement. "You have to think on a different line or physically get involved. You have to start doing something." Consider Linda, who said when working hard to fight a sullen mood: "I'm on a sewing spree. I can work on my wardrobe and, in time, I forget about what's troubling me. It really helps." Doing things that you are good at can build your self-esteem—which is usually at rock bottom during depression.

Also beneficial is engaging in activities that bring you pleasure. Try shopping for some personal treat, playing games, cooking your favorite recipe, browsing through a bookstore, dining out, reading, even working at a puzzle, such as those that appear in *Awake!* magazine.

Debbie found that by planning short trips or setting little goals for herself, she could cope with her depressed mood. However, doing things to aid others proved to be one of her biggest helps. "I met this young woman who was very depressed, and I began to help her to study the Bible," revealed Debbie. "These weekly discussions gave me opportunity to tell her how she could overcome her depression. The Bible gave her real hope. This helped me at the same time." Just as Jesus said: "There is more happiness in giving than there is in receiving."—Acts 20:35.

> *A personal friendship with God can help you to deal with major depression*

Talk to Someone About It

"Anxious care in the heart of a man is what will cause it to bow down, but the good word is what makes it rejoice." (Proverbs 12:25) A "good word" from an understanding person can make all the difference in the world. No human can read your heart, so pour it out to someone you trust who has the ability to help. "A friend is loving at all times, and becomes a brother in times of trouble," according to Proverbs 17:17. (*The Bible in Basic English*) "When you keep it to yourself it is like carrying a heavy load all alone," said 22-year-old Evan. "But when you share it with someone who is qualified to help, it becomes much lighter."

'But I've already tried that,' you may say, 'and all I

get is a lecture to look on the bright side of life.' Where, then, can you find someone who will be not only an understanding listener but also an objective counselor? —Proverbs 27:5, 6.

Finding Help

Begin by 'giving your heart to' your parents. (Proverbs 23:26) They know you better than anyone else does, and they can often help if you let them. If they discern the problem is severe, they might even arrange for you to receive professional help.*

Members of the Christian congregation are another source of help. "Over the years I had put up such a pretext that no one really knew how depressed I was," revealed Marie. "But then I confided in one of the older women in the congregation. She was so understanding! She had gone through some of the same experiences I had. So I was encouraged to realize that other people have gone through things like this and have come out just fine."

No, Marie's depression did not clear up immediately. But gradually she began to cope with her emotions as she deepened her relationship with God. Among Jehovah's true worshipers you too can find friends and "family" who are genuinely interested in your welfare. —Mark 10:29, 30; John 13:34, 35.

Power Beyond What Is Normal

The most powerful aid in dispelling gloom, however, is what the apostle Paul called "the power beyond what is normal," which comes from God. (2 Corinthians 4:7) He can help you fight off depression if you lean on him.

---

* Most medical experts advise that victims of major depression should receive professional help because of the danger of suicide. For example, there may be a need for medication that can only be dispensed by a medical professional.

(Psalm 55:22) With his holy spirit he gives power beyond your normal resources.

This friendship with God is truly reassuring. "When I have sad times," said a young woman named Georgia, "I pray a lot. I know that Jehovah is going to provide a way out no matter how deep a problem I have." Daphne agrees, adding: "You can tell Jehovah everything. You just pour out your heart and you know, even if no human can, he really understands you and cares about you."

So if you are depressed, pray to God, and seek out someone wise and understanding to whom you can bare your feelings. In the Christian congregation you will find "older men" who are skillful counselors. (James 5:14, 15) They stand ready to help you maintain your friendship with God. For God understands and invites you to throw your anxieties upon him "because he cares for you." (1 Peter 5:6, 7) Indeed, the Bible promises: "The peace of God that excels all thought will guard your hearts and your mental powers by means of Christ Jesus."—Philippians 4:7.

Questions for Discussion   Chapter 13

□ *What are some things that can cause a youth to become depressed? Have you ever felt that way?*

□ *Can you identify the symptoms of low-grade chronic depression?*

□ *Do you know how to recognize major depression? Why is this such a serious malady?*

□ *Name some ways of battling the blues. Have any of these suggestions worked for you?*

□ *Why is it so important to talk matters out when you are seriously depressed?*

Chapter 14

How Can I Make My Loneliness Go Away?

It is Saturday night. The boy sits alone in his room.

"I hate weekends!" he shouts. But there is no one in the room to answer. He picks up a magazine and sees a picture of a group of young people at the beach. He hurls the magazine against the wall. Tears well up. He clamps his teeth on his underlip, but the tears keep pushing. Unable to fight it any longer, he falls on his bed, sobbing, "Why am I always left out?"

DO YOU sometimes feel like that—cut off from the world, lonely, useless, and empty? If so, do not despair. For while feeling lonely is no fun, it is not some fatal disease. Simply put, loneliness is a warning signal. Hunger warns you that you need food. Loneliness warns you that you need companionship, closeness, intimacy. We need food to function well. Likewise, we need companionship to feel well.

Have you ever watched a bed of glowing coals? When you take one coal away from the heap, the glow of that single coal dies away. But after you put the coal back into the heap, it glows again! In isolation, we humans similarly do not "glow," or function well, for long. The need for companionship is built into our makeup.

Alone But Not Lonely

Essayist Henry David Thoreau wrote: "I never found the companion that was so companionable as solitude." Do you agree? "Yes," says Bill, age 20. "I like nature. Sometimes I get in my little boat and go out on a lake. I sit there for hours all alone. It gives me time to reflect on what I'm doing with my life. It's really great." Twenty-one-year-old Steven agrees. "I live in a big apartment building," he says, "and sometimes I go to the roof of the building just to be alone. I get some thinking done and pray. It's refreshing."

Yes, if used well, moments of solitude can give us deep satisfaction. Jesus too enjoyed such moments: "Early in the morning, while it was still dark, [Jesus] rose up and went outside and left for a lonely place, and there he began praying." (Mark 1:35) Remember, Jehovah did not say, 'It is not good for man to be momentarily by himself.' Rather, God said that it was not good for man "to *continue* by himself." (Genesis 2:18-23) It is prolonged periods of isolation, then, that may lead to loneliness. The Bible warns: "One isolating himself will seek his own selfish longing; against all practical wisdom he will break forth."—Proverbs 18:1.

Temporary Loneliness

Sometimes loneliness is imposed on us by circumstances beyond our control, like being away from close

Friends can keep in touch even across long distances

friends as a result of moving to a new location. Recalls Steven: "Back home James and I were friends, closer than brothers. When I moved away, I knew I was going to miss him." Steven pauses, as if reliving the moment of departure. "When I had to board the plane, I got choked up. We hugged, and I left. I felt that something precious was gone."

How did Steven make out in his new environment? "It was rough," he says. "Back home my friends liked me, but here some of the folks I worked with made me feel as if I were no good. I remember looking at the clock and counting back four hours (that was the time difference) and thinking what James and I could be doing right now. I felt lonely."

When things are not going well, we often dwell on better times that we had in the past. However, the Bible says: "Do not say: 'Why has it happened that the former days proved to be better than these?'" (Ecclesiastes 7:10) Why this advice?

For one thing, circumstances can change for the better. That is why researchers often speak of "temporary loneliness." Steven could thus overcome his loneliness. How? "Talking about my feelings with someone who cares helped. You cannot live on in the past. I forced myself to meet other people, show interest in them. It worked; I found new friends." And what about James? 'I was wrong. Moving away did not end our friendship. The other day I phoned him. We talked and talked for one hour and 15 minutes.'

Chronic Loneliness

Sometimes, though, the gnawing pain of loneliness persists, and there seems to be no way out. Ronny, a high school student, relates: "I've been going to school in this district for eight years, but in all that time I've never managed to make one single friend! . . . Nobody knows what I feel and nobody cares. Sometimes I think I just can't stand it anymore!"

Like Ronny, many teenagers experience what is often called chronic loneliness. This is more serious than temporary loneliness. In fact, say researchers, the two are "as different as the common cold and pneumonia." But just as pneumonia can be cured, chronic loneliness can be beaten too. The first step is trying to understand its cause. (Proverbs 1:5) And 16-year-old Rhonda pinpoints the most common cause of chronic loneliness, saying: "I think the reason why I feel very lonely is because—well you can't have friends if you feel badly

*P*eriods of solitude can be enjoyable

about yourself. And I guess I don't like myself very much."—*Lonely in America.*

Rhonda's loneliness comes from within. Her low self-esteem forms a barrier that keeps her from opening up and making friends. Says one researcher: "Thoughts such as 'I'm unattractive,' 'I'm uninteresting,' 'I'm worthless,' are common themes among the chronically lonely." The key to overcoming your loneliness may thus lie in building your self-respect. (See Chapter 12.) As you develop what the Bible calls "the new personality," characterized by kindness, lowliness of mind, and mildness, your self-respect is sure to grow!—Colossians 3:9-12.

> *'The best advice for a lonely person,' says the U.S. National Institute of Mental Health, is to 'get involved with other people'*

Furthermore, as you learn to like yourself, others will be drawn to your appealing qualities. But just as you can only see the full colors of a flower after it unfolds, so others can fully appreciate your qualities only if you open up to them.

Breaking the Ice

'The best advice for a lonely person,' says a recent publication from the U.S. National Institute of Mental Health, is to 'get involved with other people.' This advice harmonizes with the Bible's counsel to "widen out" and show "fellow feeling," or empathy. (2 Corinthians 6:11-13; 1 Peter 3:8) It works. Caring for others not only gets your mind off your own loneliness but motivates others to take an interest in *you.*

Nineteen-year-old Natalie thus decided that she would do more than sit back and wait for people to say hi. 'I have to be friendly too,' she says. 'Otherwise people will think I'm stuck-up.' So start with a smile. The other person might smile back.

Next, strike up a conversation. Lillian, age 15, admits: "Going up to strangers for the first time was really scary. I was afraid that they wouldn't accept me." How does Lillian start conversations? She says: "I ask simple questions like, 'Where are you from?' 'Do you know so and so?' We both may know a person, and before long we're talking." Kind acts and a generous spirit will likewise help you to build precious friendships.—Proverbs 11:25.

Remember too that you can have a friend who will never let you down. Jesus Christ told his disciples: "I am not alone, because the Father is with me." (John 16:32) Jehovah can become your closest friend too. Get to know his personality by reading the Bible and observing his creation. Strengthen your friendship with him by prayer. Ultimately, a friendship with Jehovah God is the best cure for loneliness.

If you still feel lonely from time to time, relax. That is perfectly normal. What, though, if extreme shyness is holding you back from making friends and being with others?

Questions for Discussion   *Chapter 14*

□ *Is being alone necessarily a bad thing? Are there benefits from solitude?*

□ *Why is most loneliness temporary? Have you found this to be true in your own case?*

□ *What is chronic loneliness, and how can you battle it?*

□ *What are some ways of 'breaking the ice' with others? What has worked for you?*

Chapter 15

Why Am I So Shy?

"EVERYONE tells me how great-looking I am," wrote a young woman to a newspaper column. Yet she went on to state: "I have a problem talking to people. If I look someone in the eyes while speaking, my face turns red and I get all choked up inside . . . At work I have heard several comments on how 'stuck up' I am because I don't talk to anybody. . . . I'm not stuck up, I'm just shy."

The shy person misses out on friendships and opportunities

One survey showed that 80 percent of those questioned had been shy at some time in their life, and 40 percent currently considered themselves to be shy. Indeed, shyness has been common with mankind from earliest times. The Bible tells us that Moses shyly declined to act as God's spokesman before the nation of Israel. (Exodus 3:11, 13; 4:1, 10, 13) It appears, too, that the Christian disciple Timothy was shy and diffident about speaking up and properly exercising his authority.—1 Timothy 4:12; 2 Timothy 1: 6-8.

What Shyness Is

Shyness is feeling uneasy around people—strangers, those in authority, persons of the opposite sex, or even your peers. It is extreme self-consciousness that affects its victims in a variety of ways. Some get embarrassed; with eyes downcast and heart pounding, they find themselves unable to speak. Others lose their composure and begin to chatter continuously. Yet others find it hard to speak up and voice their opinions or preferences.

Actually, though, there are positive aspects to having a measure of shyness. It is akin to modesty and humility, and one of the things God looks for and commends is 'being modest in walking with him.' (Micah 6:8) There is further benefit in appearing discreet and unassuming, in not being overbearing and overly aggressive. A shy person is often valued as a good listener. But when shyness restricts and inhibits us from realizing our full potential and harmfully affects our relationships, work, and feelings, it is time to do something about it!

A good start is understanding the problem. (Proverbs 1:5) Shyness does not describe what you are; it describes your behavior, your reaction to situations, the pattern you have learned and reinforced through experiences with others. You *think* others are making negative judgments of you, that they don't like you. You *think* others are better or more normal than you. You *think* things will go all wrong if you try to relate to other people. You expect things to turn out badly, and they often do—because you tense up and act in harmony with your beliefs.

How Shyness Affects Your Life

By withdrawing, not speaking up, or being so preoccupied with self that you don't pay attention to others, you may leave the impression that you are stuck-up, unfriendly, bored, or even uncaring or ignorant. When your thoughts are on yourself, it is hard to concentrate on the discussion at hand. So you pay less attention to the information you are receiving. Then what you fear most happens—you appear foolish.

In essence, you have locked yourself behind the

The shy person imagines that others think little of him

walls of the prison of shyness and have thrown away the key. You let opportunities pass you by. You accept items or situations you really don't want—all because you are afraid to speak up and express your opinion. You lose out on the joys of meeting people and making new friends or of doing things that would enhance your life. But others lose out too. They never get to know the real you.

Overcoming Shyness

With time and effort, behavior can be changed. First of all, stop worrying about whether the other person is evaluating you. He is probably too busy thinking of himself and what *he* will say and do. And if that person childishly pokes fun at you, understand that *he* has the problem. "He who belittles his neighbor lacks sense." (Proverbs 11:12, *Revised Standard Version*) Those who are worth having as friends will judge not by outward appearances but by the kind of person you are.

Also, try to think positively. No one is perfect; all of us have our strengths and our weaknesses. Remember, there are different ways of looking at things, different likes and dislikes. A difference of opinion does not mean a rejection of you as a person.

Learn also to judge others fairly. One formerly shy

You can overcome shyness by

Wanting to change and believing that change is really possible

Replacing negative thoughts with positive action

Setting realistic and meaningful goals for yourself

Knowing how to relax and cope with anxiety

Rehearsing a situation beforehand

Gaining confidence by progressively successful experiences

Remembering that differences of opinion exist and that others err too

Practicing to increase skills and learn new ones

Reaching out to show love and to help others

Dressing tastefully and acting with confidence

Relying on the help that God gives

Being involved with Christian meetings and in sharing your faith with others

young man says: "I discovered two things about myself . . . First, I was too self-centered. I was thinking too much about myself, worrying about what people thought of what I said. Second, I was assigning bad motives to the other persons—not trusting them and thinking they were going to look down on me."

The young man attended a meeting of Jehovah's Witnesses. "I heard a talk there that really helped me," he recalls. 'The speaker pointed out that love is outgoing; that if you have love you think the best of people, not the worst. So I learned to quit assigning bad motives to people. I told myself: "They're going to be understanding, they're going to be kind, they're going to be considerate." I began to trust people. I realized that some might misjudge me, but I now felt that that was *their* problem.'

YOUNG PEOPLE ASK . . .

"I also learned the need to start showing love in an active way—to extend myself more to others," he explained. "I tried it first on younger ones. Later I began visiting others in their homes. I learned to be sensitive to their needs, to think in terms of helping them." Thus he learned the truthfulness of Jesus' counsel at Luke 6:37, 38: "Stop judging, and you will by no means be judged; and stop condemning, and you will by no means be condemned. . . . Practice giving, and people will give to you. . . . For with the measure that you are measuring out, they will measure out to you in return."

Making a Start

So learn to be sociable—to say hello and start a conversation. It can be as simple as a comment on the weather. Remember: You have only 50 percent of the responsibility. The other half is up to the other person. If you blunder in speech, don't feel condemned. If others laugh, learn to laugh with them. Saying "That didn't come out right" will help you to relax and continue with the conversation.

Dress comfortably, but make sure that your clothes are clean and pressed. Feeling that you are looking your best will minimize apprehension in this regard and enable you to concentrate on the conversation at hand.

Learn to be sociable—to smile, greet others, and carry on a conversation

Stand straight—yet be at ease. Look pleasant and smile. Maintain friendly eye contact and nod or verbally acknowledge what the other person says.

When facing a tough situation, such as a speech in front of others or a job interview, come as prepared as possible. Practice beforehand what you will say. Speech problems can also be overcome or minimized by practice. It will take time, just as it does to acquire any other set of new skills. But as you see the positive results, you will be further encouraged to succeed.

Not to be overlooked is the help that God can give. Saul, the first king of the ancient nation of Israel, was painfully shy at first. (1 Samuel, chapters 9 and 10) But when the time came for action, "the spirit of God became operative upon Saul," and he led the people to victory!—1 Samuel, chapter 11.

Today Christian youths have the responsibility to help others learn about God and his promised new world of righteousness. (Matthew 24:14) Carrying this good news and representing the highest Authority in the universe is sure to inspire self-confidence and to help one get the focus off oneself. You can be sure, then, that if you faithfully serve God, he will bless you and help you overcome your shyness.

Questions for Discussion   *Chapter 15*

□ *Just what is shyness, and how does a shy person behave in the presence of others? Is this true of you to some extent?*

□ *Why does a shy person lose confidence when he is around others?*

□ *How can shyness cause a person to suffer loss?*

□ *What are some ways of overcoming shyness? Have any of these suggestions worked for you?*

Chapter 16

Is It Normal to Grieve the Way I Do?

MITCHELL recalls the day his dad died: "I was in a state of shock. . . . 'It can't be true,' I kept telling myself."

Perhaps someone you love—a parent, a brother, a sister, or a friend—has died. And rather than feel only sorrow, you also feel anger, confusion, and fear. Try as you may, you can't hold back tears. Or you keep the pain you feel bottled up inside.

Really, it is only natural to react emotionally when someone we love dies. Even Jesus Christ, when he learned of the death of a close friend, "gave way to tears" and "groaned" inside. (John 11:33-36; compare 2 Samuel 13:28-39.) Realizing that others have felt as you do may help you better to deal with your loss.

Denial

At first you may feel numb. Perhaps deep inside you hope that it's all just a bad dream, that someone will come and wake you up and things will be just as they've always been. Cindy's mother, for example, died of cancer. Explains Cindy: "I've not really accepted that she's gone. Something will happen that I might have discussed with her in the past, and I find myself saying, 'I'll have to tell Mom that.'"

Bereaved persons tend to deny that the death has occurred. They may even think they suddenly see the deceased one on the street, in a passing bus, on the subway. Any fleeting resemblance can spark the hope that perhaps it has all been a mistake. Remember, God made man to live, not to die. (Genesis 1:28; 2:9) So it's only normal that we have trouble accepting death.

"How Could She Do That to Me?"

Don't be surprised if there are even moments when you feel a little angry with the person who died. Cindy recalls: "When Mom died, there were times when I thought, 'You really didn't let us know you were going to die. You just skipped out.' I felt deserted."

The death of a brother or a sister can likewise stir

> *"I've not really accepted that she's gone. . . . I find myself saying, 'I'll have to tell Mom that' "*

such feelings. "It's almost ridiculous to feel anger at someone who's died," explains Karen, "but when my sister died, I couldn't help it. Thoughts like, 'How could she die and leave me all alone? How could she do that to me?' kept going through my head." Some find themselves angry at the sibling for all the pain that his or her death has caused. Some feel neglected, perhaps even resentful, because of all the time and attention that the sick brother or sister received before dying. Grief-stricken parents who, out of fear of losing another child, suddenly become overly protective can also stir animosity toward the deceased.

"If only . . . "

Guilt is also a frequent reaction. Questions and doubts pour through the mind. 'Is there anything more we could have done? Should we have consulted another doctor?' And then there are the *if onlys*. 'If only we had not quarreled so much.' 'If only I had been kinder.' 'If only I had gone to the store, instead.'

YOUNG PEOPLE ASK . . .

"This isn't really happening to me!"

Mitchell says: "I wish I had been more patient and understanding with my father. Or done more things around the house to make it easier for him when he came home." And Elisa observed: "When Mom got sick and died so suddenly, there were all of these unresolved feelings we'd had for each other. I feel so guilty now. I think of all the things I should have said to her, all the things I shouldn't have said, all the things I did wrong."

You may even blame yourself for what happened. Cindy recalls: "I felt guilty over every argument we ever had, over all the stress I caused Mom. I felt that all the stress I caused her could have contributed to her illness."

"What Do I Tell My Friends?"

One widow observed regarding her son: "Jonny hated to tell other children that his father was dead. It embarrassed him and it also made him angry, just because he was embarrassed."

When we lose someone we love in death, we need the support of someone compassionate

The book *Death and Grief in the Family* explains: "'What do I tell my friends?' is a question of supreme importance to many siblings [surviving brothers or sisters]. Frequently, siblings feel that their friends do not understand what they are experiencing. Attempts to share the import of the loss may be met with blank stares and quizzical looks. . . . Consequently, the bereaved sibling may feel rejected, isolated, and, at times, even freakish."

Realize, though, that others sometimes simply do not know what to say to a grieving friend—and so they say nothing. Your loss may also remind them that they, too, can lose a loved one. Not wanting to be reminded of that, they may shy away from you.

Facing Up to Your Grief

Knowing that your grief is normal is a big help in coming to grips with it. But it only prolongs grief to continue to deny reality. Sometimes a family will leave a vacant place at the meal table for the deceased, as if that one were about to come in for a meal. One family, though, chose to handle matters differently. Says the mother: "We never sat at the kitchen table in the same order anymore. My husband moved into David's chair, and that helped to fill that void."

It also helps to realize that while there may well be things you should or shouldn't have said or done, usually those are *not* the reasons your loved one died. Besides, "We all stumble many times."—James 3:2.

Sharing Your Feelings

Dr. Earl Grollman suggests: "It is not enough to recognize your conflicting emotions; you must deal with them openly. . . . This is a time to share your feelings." It is not a time to isolate yourself.—Proverbs 18:1.

Dr. Grollman says that in denying grief, "you only prolong the agony and delay the grief process." He suggests: "Find a good listener, a friend who will understand that your many feelings are *normal* reactions to your bitter grief." A

> *"When Mom died, . . . I thought, 'You really didn't let us know you were going to die. You just skipped out.' I felt deserted"*

parent, a brother, a sister, a friend, or an elder in the Christian congregation can often prove to be a real support.

And what if you feel like weeping? Dr. Grollman adds: "For some, tears are the best therapy for emotional strain, for men as well as for women and children. Weeping is a natural way to ease anguish and release pain."

Pulling Together as a Family

Your parents can also be a great help in time of loss —and you can be a help to them. For example, Jane and Sarah, from England, lost their 23-year-old brother Darrall. How did they survive their grief? Jane answers:

"Because there were four of us, I went and did everything with Dad, whilst Sarah did everything with Mum. In this way we were not on our own." Jane further recalls: "I had never seen Dad cry before. He cried a couple of times, and in a way, it was nice, and looking back, I feel good now that I could be there just to comfort him."

A Hope That Sustains

Young David, from England, lost his 13-year-old sister Janet to Hodgkin's disease. He says: "One of the things that benefited me greatly was one text quoted in the funeral talk. It states: 'Because God has set a day in which he purposes to judge the inhabited earth in righteousness, and he has furnished a guarantee to all men in that he has resurrected him, Jesus, from the dead.' The speaker stressed the expression 'guarantee' concerning the resurrection. That was a great source of strength to me after the funeral."—Acts 17:31; see also Mark 5:35-42; 12:26, 27; John 5:28, 29; 1 Corinthians 15:3-8.

The Bible's hope of the resurrection does not eliminate grief. You will never forget your loved one. However, many have found real comfort in the Bible's promises and, as a result, have begun to recover gradually from the pain of losing someone they loved.

Questions for Discussion   *Chapter 16*

□ *Do you feel it is natural to grieve for someone you love who has died?*

□ *What emotions might a grieving person experience, and why?*

□ *What are some ways a grieving youth can begin to come to grips with his or her feelings?*

□ *How might you comfort a friend who has lost a loved one?*

School and Work

*S*chool, love it or hate it, is where you will probably spend about 12 years of your life. These can be years of drudgery or of discovery. Much depends upon how you use those school years. In this section we will therefore take an in-depth look at school, homework, grades, and teachers. And for those of you already out of school, we have some solid tips for survival in the job market.

Chapter 17

Should I Quit School?

JACK has been a school attendance officer for over 25 years. A truant youth is therefore hard pressed to come up with an excuse Jack has not already heard. "I've been told everything by the kids," he says, "such as 'I thought I was going to be sick today' . . . 'My grandfather in Alaska died.'" Jack's "favorite" excuse? It was from three boys who claimed they "couldn't find the school because it was too foggy."

These embarrassingly shaky alibis illustrate the aversion many youths have toward school, often ranging from indifference ("It's all right, I guess") to outright hostility ("School stinks! I hate it"). Gary, for example, would get up for school and immediately feel sick to his stomach. Said he, "I'd get close to the school, and I'd get so sweaty and nervous . . . I just had to get back to my house." Many youths similarly suffer an obsessive dread of school—something doctors call school phobia. It is often triggered by school violence, peer cruelty, and pressure to get good grades. Such youths may (with a bit of parental persuasion) go to school, but they suffer constant turmoil and even physical distress.

Not surprisingly an alarming number of youths choose not to go to school at all! In the United States alone, some two and a half million students of elementary and secondary schools are absent every day! An article in *The New York Times* added that so many (about one third) are "chronically absent" in New York City high schools "that it is nearly impossible to teach them."

Other youths are taking yet more drastic steps.

"School was boring, too strict," said a young man named Walter. He dropped out of high school (secondary school). So did a girl named Antonia. She was having difficulty with her schoolwork. "How could I do the work if I didn't understand what I was reading?" she asked. "I was just sitting there getting dumber and dumber, so I left."

Admittedly, serious problems plague school systems around the world. But is this reason to lose all interest in school and drop out? What effects might dropping out have on your life later on? Are there good reasons for staying in school until you graduate?

The Value of an Education

Michael returned to school to get a high school equivalency diploma. When asked why, he said, "I realized that I needed an education." But just what is an "education"? The ability to recite an impressive array of facts? This no more makes an education than a pile of bricks makes a house.

Education should prepare you for a successful adult life. Allen Austill, a school dean for 18 years, spoke of "the education that teaches you how to think, to solve problems, what is rational and irrational, the fundamental capacity to think clearly, to know what data is and to know the connections between parts and whole. To make those judgments and distinctions, to learn how to learn."

> *"I was just sitting there getting dumber and dumber, so I left"*

And how does school fit in? Centuries ago King Solomon wrote proverbs "to give to the inexperienced ones shrewdness, to a young man knowledge and thinking ability." (Proverbs 1:1-4) Yes, inexperience

The discipline you learn in school can benefit you for the rest of your life

goes with youth. School, however, can help you nurture and cultivate thinking ability. This is the ability not merely to recite facts but also to analyze them and generate productive ideas from them. Though many have criticized the way some schools go about teaching, school *does* force you to use your mind. True, solving geometry problems or memorizing a list of historical dates may not seem relevant to your life at the time. But as Barbara Mayer wrote in *The High School Survival Guide:* "Not everyone is going to remember all the facts and bits of knowledge which teachers like to put in tests, but the skills such as learning how to study, and how to plan, will never be forgotten."

Three university professors who studied the long-term effects of education similarly concluded that "the better educated do have wider and deeper knowledge not merely of bookish facts but also of the contemporary world, and that they are more likely to seek out knowledge and be attuned to sources of information. . . . These differences are found to have endured despite aging and many years of removal from school."—*The Enduring Effects of Education.*

Most important of all, an education can equip you to carry out your Christian responsibilities. If you have acquired good study habits and have mastered the art of reading, you can more easily study God's Word. (Psalm 1:2) Having learned in school to express yourself, you can more easily teach Bible truths to others. A knowledge of history, science, geography, and math is likewise useful and will help you to relate to people of various backgrounds, interests, and beliefs.

School and Employment

School also has a great impact on your future employment prospects. How so?

Job prospects are dim for those who haven't mastered the basic skills taught in school

Wise King Solomon said of the skillful worker: "Before kings is where he will station himself; he will not station himself before commonplace men." (Proverbs 22:29) This is still true today. "Without skills, a lot of things in life can leave you behind," said Ernest Green of the U.S. Department of Labor.

Understandably, then, the job outlook for those who quit school is poor. Walter (quoted earlier) learned this the hard way. "A lot of times I've applied for jobs and I couldn't get them because I didn't have a diploma." He also admitted: "Sometimes people use words I can't understand, and I feel stupid."

> *"A recent study indicates that it takes approximately a seventh-grade reading level to hold a job as a cook, an eighth-grade level to hold a job as a mechanic, and a ninth- or tenth-grade level to hold a job as a supply clerk"*

Unemployment among 16- to 24-year-olds who are high school dropouts "is nearly twice that of their peers who did graduate and nearly three times that of the overall unemployment rate." (*The New York Times*) "Those who do not continue their education are closing the doors to opportunity," adds author F. Philip Rice in his book *The Adolescent.* Someone who has dropped out has likely not mastered the basic skills needed to handle the simplest of jobs.

Paul Copperman writes in his book *The Literacy Hoax:* "A recent study indicates that it takes approximately a seventh-grade reading level to hold a job as a cook, an eighth-grade level to hold a job as a mechanic, and a ninth- or tenth-grade level to hold a job as a supply clerk." He continues: "I believe it is a reasonable inference that a job as a teacher, nurse, accountant, or engineer would demand a higher minimum level of reading ability."

Obviously, then, the students who really apply themselves to learning basic skills, such as reading, will have far better job opportunities. But what is another lifelong benefit that can be derived from attending school?

A Better You

That lifelong benefit is your knowing your strengths and weaknesses. Michelle, who recently took a job in the computer field, observed: "In school I learned how to work under pressure, how to take a test and how to express myself."

'School taught me how to view failure,' says another youth. She had the tendency to view others, and not herself, as the cause of her setbacks. Others have benefited from the disciplined school routine. Many criticize the schools because of this, claiming that this stifles young minds. Yet Solomon encouraged youths "to know wisdom and discipline." (Proverbs 1:2) Schools in which discipline prevails have indeed produced many disciplined, yet creative, minds.

It therefore makes good sense for you to take full advantage of your school years. How can you do that? Let's start with your schoolwork itself.

Questions for Discussion   Chapter 17

☐ *Why do so many youths have a negative view of school? How do you feel about the matter?*

☐ *How does school help a person develop thinking ability?*

☐ *How might dropping out of school affect your future ability to get a job, and why?*

☐ *What other personal benefits may result from staying in school?*

Chapter 18

How Can I Improve My Grades?

WHEN a number of elementary school students were asked, 'What do you worry about most?' 51 percent said, "Grades"!

Little wonder that school grades are a major source of anxiety among youths. Grades can mean the difference between graduating and being left behind, between obtaining a well-paying job and getting only a minimum wage, between receiving the praise of parents and incurring their wrath. Admittedly, grades and tests have their place. Why, Jesus Christ often tested his disciples' understanding of certain matters. (Luke 9:18) And as the book *Measurement and Evaluation in the Schools* says: "Test results can reveal areas of strength and weakness of individual students and act as motivating devices for future study." Your grades also serve to give your parents some idea of how you are doing in school—for better or for worse.

Finding the Balance

Too much concern about grades, however, can create paralyzing stresses and ignite fierce competition. One textbook on adolescence observes that college-bound students can especially be "caught up in a competitive maze that emphasizes grades and class rank rather than learning." As a result, to quote Dr. William Glasser, students "learn early in school to ask what is going to be on the test and . . . study only that material."

Warned King Solomon: "I myself have seen all the

hard work and all the proficiency in work, that it means the rivalry of one toward another; this also is vanity and a striving after the wind." (Ecclesiastes 4:4) Fierce competition, whether for material riches or academic accolades, is futile. God-fearing youths see the need to apply themselves in school. But instead of making education the most important thing in life, they pursue spiritual interests, trusting God to care for their material needs. —Matthew 6:33; see Chapter 22 on choosing careers.

Furthermore, education means more than racking up points on tests. It means developing what Solomon called "thinking ability," the skill of taking raw information and drawing sound, practical conclusions from it. (Proverbs 1:4) A youth who manages to get passing grades through guessing, cramming, or even cheating never really learns how to think. And what good is a high grade in math if later on you find yourself unable to balance a checkbook?

A youth who manages to get passing grades through guessing, cramming, or even cheating never really learns how to think

It is thus important that you view grades, not as an end in themselves, but as a helpful means of gauging your progress at school. How, though, can you achieve grades that reflect your abilities?

Take Responsibility for Learning!

According to teacher Linda Nielsen, poor students tend to "blame their poor [school] performances on sources beyond their control: unfair test questions, a prejudiced teacher, bad luck, fate, the weather." The Bible, though, says: "The lazy one is showing himself desirous, but his soul has nothing." (Proverbs 13:4) Yes, laziness is often the real reason for low grades.

Good students, however, take responsibility for their learning. *'Teen* magazine once polled some high-achieving high (secondary) school students. Their secret? "Personal motivation helps you keep going," said one. "Putting yourself on a schedule and organizing your time," said another. "You have to set goals for yourself," said yet another. Yes, how good your grades are depends for the most part, not on factors beyond your control, but on YOU—how hard you are willing to study and apply yourself in school.

'But I *Do* Study'

This is what some youths might claim. They sincerely feel they are already working themselves to the bone but getting no results. A few years ago, however, researchers at Stanford University (U.S.A.) polled some 770 students and asked how much effort they felt they were putting into their schoolwork. Oddly enough, students with low grades thought they worked as hard as anybody! Yet when their study habits were examined, it was discovered that they actually did far less homework than their high-achieving schoolmates.

The lesson? Perhaps you too are not studying as hard as you think you are, and some changes would be in order. An article in the *Journal of Educational Psychology* showed that simply making "an increase in time spent on homework has a positive effect on a student's grades in high school." In fact, "with 1 to 3 hours of homework a week, the average low ability student can achieve grades commensurate with an average ability student who does not do homework."

The apostle Paul figuratively had to 'pummel his body' to reach his goals. (1 Corinthians 9:27) You may similarly have to institute a get-tough policy with yourself, especially if TV or other distractions easily divert your attention from studying. You might even try putting a sign on the TV that says, "No TV until homework is done!"

Your Study Environment

Most of us would benefit from having a quiet place that is set aside for study. If you share a room or if space is limited in your home, improvise! Perhaps the kitchen or someone's bedroom can be proclaimed your study area for an hour or so each evening. Or as a last resort, try a public library or a friend's home.

If possible, use a desk or a table with plenty of space on which to spread out your work. Keep supplies such as pencils and paper handy so you won't have to get up constantly. And, sorry to say, having the TV or the radio on generally works *against* concentration, as do telephone calls or visiting.

Make sure, too, that you have adequate, glare-free lighting. Good lighting reduces study fatigue and protects your eyes as well. And if possible, check ventilation and room temperature. A cool room provides a

Students often pay for loose study habits . . . with failing grades

What About Afterschool Activities?

Many young people find that afterschool activities give them a sense of accomplishment. "I was into just about every club there was," recalls one boy from Baltimore, Maryland (U.S.A.). "It made me feel good to work with things I like. I was in an automotive club because I enjoy working with cars. I like computers, so I joined that club. I like audio, so I joined that club." College-bound students are particularly urged to participate in afterschool activities.

However, a U.S. federal government official—formerly a teacher himself—told <u>Awake!</u>: "Probably the students spend more time with extracurricular activities than with schoolwork, making it hard to maintain grades." Yes, it is not easy to maintain balance when it comes to extracurricular activities. Says a girl named Cathy who used to play on the school softball team: "After the practice, I was too tired to do anything else. My schoolwork was affected. So I did not sign up this year."

There are also spiritual dangers. Says one Christian man looking back on his teen years: "I thought I could harmonize three activities: schoolwork, practice with the track team, and spiritual activities. But the spiritual aspect of my life was sacrificed whenever the three conflicted."

more invigorating study environment than a warm room does.

What if you are simply not in the mood for studying? Life seldom allows us the luxury of indulging our moods. At a secular job, you will have to work every day —whether you are in the mood for it or not. So view

Young Themon, who was involved in two sports teams at school, agrees: "I could not attend meetings at the [Kingdom] Hall [for spiritual instruction] because Tuesday we were out of town, Thursday we were out of town, Saturday we were out of town and would not get back until two o'clock in the morning." Though "bodily training is beneficial for a little," it is vital to remember that "godly devotion is beneficial for all things."—1 Timothy 4:8.

Think, too, of the moral dangers. Would you be associating with wholesome friends who would be a good moral influence? What would be the subject of conversation? Could the influence of teammates or members of a club have an adverse effect on you? "Bad associations spoil useful habits," says 1 Corinthians 15:33.

Interestingly, many youths among Jehovah's Witnesses have chosen to use their afterschool time for something far more beneficial than sports: helping others to know the Creator. Advises Colossians 4:5: "Go on walking in wisdom toward those on the outside, buying out the opportune time for yourselves."

homework as an exercise in self-discipline, a rehearsal for later work experience. Be businesslike about it. Suggests one educator: "If possible, studying should be done in the same place and at the same time every day. Thus, regular study will become a habit, and . . . will reduce your resistance to study."

Balancing afterschool activities with your homework is not easy

Your Study Routine

At Philippians 3:16, Paul encouraged Christians to "go on walking orderly in this same routine." Paul was speaking of the routine of Christian living. However, a routine, or pattern of doing things, is also helpful when it comes to your method of studying. Try, for instance, to organize what you are going to study. Avoid studying similar subjects (such as two foreign languages) in sequence. Plan brief breaks between subjects, especially if your homework load is heavy.

If your assignment involves a lot of reading, you might try the following method. First, SURVEY your material. Glance through the assigned material, looking at subheadings, charts, and so forth, in order to get an overall view of it. Next, make up QUESTIONS based on chapter titles or topic sentences. (This keeps your mind focused on what you read.) Now READ, looking for the answers to these questions. When you have finished each paragraph or section, RECITE, or tell yourself from memory, what you have read, without looking at the book. And when you have finished the entire assignment, REVIEW by scanning headings and testing your memory of each section. Some claim that this method has helped students retain up to 80 percent of what they read!

One educator further says: "It's important to have the student realize that a fact doesn't exist in isolation but is always related to other information." Try, therefore, to relate what you study to what you already know and have experienced. Search for the practical value of what you are learning.

Interestingly, the God-fearing youth has a real advantage here. For the Bible says: "The fear of Jehovah is the beginning of knowledge." (Proverbs 1:7) Learning the laws of physics, for example, may seem like pure drudgery. But knowing that through creation God's "invisible qualities are clearly seen" gives added meaning to what you learn. (Romans 1:20) History likewise often touches on the outworking of Jehovah's purposes. Seven world powers (including the present Anglo-American combine) are discussed right in the Bible itself!—Revelation 17:10; Daniel, chapter 7.

By relating what you learn to what you know or to your Christian faith, facts begin to mean something to you, knowledge grows into understanding. And as Solomon observed, "To the understanding one knowledge is an easy thing."—Proverbs 14:6.

'There Will Be a Test Next Week'

These words need not cause you to panic. First of all, try to discern from your teacher's comments what kind of test it will be, such as an essay test or multiple choice. Also, in the days preceding the test, listen for clues as to what will appear in the test. ("This next point

Parents are sure to be upset over a bad report card. But if you feel they are expecting too much of you, talk it over with them

is very important" or "Be sure to remember that" are typical hints, says *Senior Scholastic* magazine.) Next, review your notes, textbooks, and homework assignments.

"By iron, iron itself is sharpened. So one man sharpens the face of another," Solomon reminds us. (Proverbs 27:17) Perhaps a friend or one of your parents would be happy to drill you with questions or listen to you as you recite classroom material. And then the night before the test, relax and try to get a good night's sleep. "Who of you by being anxious can add one cubit to his life span?" Jesus asked.—Matthew 6:27.

Failure

Failing a test—especially after trying hard to pass it—can devastate your self-respect. But educator Max Rafferty reminds us: "As long as we live, we're graded on what we know, how well we get results . . . A school that kids the kids into thinking that life is going to be all Roman candles is not a school. It's a dream factory." The humiliation of failing a test may well be worth it if it spurs you on to learn from your mistakes and improve.

But what about facing disappointed parents with a bad report card? Fear of doing so has at times given birth to elaborate stall tactics. "I used to put my report card on the kitchen table, go upstairs and try to sleep till the next day," recalls one youth. "What I'd do," says another, "is wait till the last second to show it to my mother. I'd take it to her in the morning when she was just about to go to work and say, 'Here, you've got to sign this.' She didn't have time to deal with me"—at least not for the moment. Some youths have even forged phony grades on their report cards!

Your parents, though, have a right to know how you are doing in school. Naturally, they expect your grades to reflect your abilities, and if your grades are under par, you can expect to receive well-deserved discipline. So be honest with your parents. And "listen . . . to the discipline of your father, and do not forsake the law of your mother." (Proverbs 1:8) If you think too much is being expected of you, talk it over with them.—See insert entitled "How Can I Tell My Parents?" in Chapter 2.

As important as grades are, they are not the final judgment on your worth as a person. Nevertheless, take advantage of the time you are in school, and learn as much as you can. Usually that effort will be reflected in grades that will make you—and your parents—feel happy and satisfied.

Questions for Discussion   Chapter 18

- □ *What purpose do grades serve, and why is it important to have a balanced view of them?*
- □ *Why is it important that you take personal responsibility for learning?*
- □ *What are some things to consider about taking on afterschool activities?*
- □ *What are some ways in which you can improve your grades?*
- □ *How can you prepare for tests?*
- □ *How should you view failure, and should such failure be concealed from your parents?*

Chapter 19

Why Won't the Kids Leave Me Alone?

The boy's walk is a dead giveaway. Tense and unsure of himself, he is obviously bewildered by his new surroundings. The older students immediately spot him as a new kid in school. Within moments he is surrounded by youths who begin assailing him with obscenities! Crimson from ear to ear, he flees to the nearest sanctuary—the rest room. Laughter echoes off the walls.

HARASSING, teasing, and insulting others are the cruel pastimes of many young ones. Even in Bible times, some youths manifested a mean streak. For example, a group of young boys once harassed the prophet Elisha. Showing contempt for his office, the youths disrespectfully cried out: "Go up, you baldhead! Go up, you baldhead!" (2 Kings 2:23-25) Today, many youths are similarly inclined to make insulting, hurtful remarks about others.

"I was the runt of my ninth-grade class," recalls one of the authors of *Growing Pains in the Classroom*. "Being the smartest kid and the shortest kid in the room was a disaster combination for junior high: those who didn't want to hit me for being a runt hit me for being a smart guy. In addition to 'four eyes,' I was called 'a walking dictionary,' and 800 other epithets [abusive words]." The author of *The Loneliness of Children* adds: "Children with physical handicaps, speech problems, or obvious physical or behavioral peculiarities are ready targets for teasing by other children."

Sometimes youths defend themselves by joining in what amounts to a cruel contest: firing increasingly hurtful insults (often regarding the other's parents) at one another. But many youths are defenseless in the face of peer harassment. One youth recalls that some days, because of teasing and harassment by fellow classmates, he was so scared and unhappy that he 'thought he would vomit.' He couldn't concentrate on his studies for worrying about what the other students would do to him.

No Laughing Matter

Have you been the butt of peer cruelty? Then you may be comforted to know that God does not view it as a laughing matter. Consider the Bible account of a feast that was arranged to celebrate the weaning of Abraham's son Isaac. Apparently jealous of the inheritance Isaac would receive, Abraham's older son, Ishmael, began "poking fun" at Isaac. Far from being good-natured fun, however, the teasing amounted to 'persecution.' (Galatians 4:29) Isaac's mother, Sarah, thus sensed hostility in the teasing. She saw it as an affront to Jehovah's purpose to produce a "seed," or Messiah, through her son, Isaac. At Sarah's request, Ishmael and his mother were dismissed from Abraham's household.—Genesis 21:8-14.

Similarly, it is no laughing matter when youths maliciously harass you—especially when they do so because you endeavor to live by Bible standards. Christian youths,

Many youths are the victims of harassment by peers

How Can I Avoid Getting Beaten Up?

'You take your life in your hands when you come to school.' So say many students. But carrying a weapon is foolish and invites trouble. (Proverbs 11:27) How, then, can you protect yourself?

Know and avoid danger spots. Hallways, stairwells, and locker rooms are real trouble spots in some schools. And so notorious are rest rooms as gathering places for fights and drug usage that many youths would rather suffer discomfort than use these facilities.

Watch your associations. Often a youth finds himself in the middle of a fight simply because he associates with the wrong crowd. (See Proverbs 22:24, 25.) Of course, giving the cold shoulder to your schoolmates could alienate them or make them hostile toward you. If you are friendly and polite to them, they may be more inclined to leave you alone.

Walk away from fights. Avoid "forcing one another to a showdown." (Galatians 5: 26, footnote) Even if you come off the victor in a fight, your opponent may simply bide his or her time for a re-match. So first try talking your way out of a fight. (Proverbs 15:1) If talking doesn't work, walk—or even run—away from a violent confrontation. Remember, "A live dog is better off than a dead lion." (Ecclesiastes 9:4) As a last resort, take whatever reasonable means are necessary to protect and defend yourself. —Romans 12:18.

Talk to your parents. Youths "seldom report their school terrors to their parents, for fear the parents will think them cowardly or chide them for not standing up to the bullies." (The Loneliness of Children) Often, though, a parent's intervention is the only way to stop the trouble.

Pray to God. God does not guarantee you will be spared physical harm. But he can give you the courage to face confrontations and the wisdom needed to cool off the situation.—James 1:5.

for example, are known for sharing their faith with others. But, as one group of young witnesses of Jehovah said: "The kids in school make fun of us because we preach from door to door, and they put us down for it." Yes, like faithful servants of God in ancient times, many Christian youths receive a "trial by mockings." (Hebrews 11:36) They are to be commended for their courage in enduring such reproaches!

Why They Do It

Nevertheless, you may wonder how to make your tormentors leave you alone. First, consider why the teasing takes place. "Even in laughter the heart may be in pain," says the Bible at Proverbs 14:13. Laughter erupts when a group of youths harass someone. But they are not 'crying out joyfully because of the good condition of the heart.' (Isaiah 65:14) Often the laughter is a mere camouflage of inner turmoil. Behind the bravado, the tormentors might really be saying: 'We don't like ourselves, but putting someone down makes us feel better.'

Jealousy also prompts the attacks. Recall the Bible's account of the teenager Joseph, whose own brothers turned on him because he was his father's favorite. Intense jealousy led not only to verbal abuse but even to the contemplation of murder! (Genesis 37:4, 11, 20) Likewise today, a student who is exceptionally bright or well liked by the teachers may arouse the jealousy of his peers. Insults seem to 'cut him down to size.'

The ridiculer wants to revel in your misery. Lashing back or bursting into tears might even encourage further harassment

Insecurity, jealousy, and low self-esteem are thus often the reasons for ridicule. Why, then, should you lose your self-esteem because some insecure youth has lost his?

Halting the Harassment

"Happy is the man that . . . in the seat of ridiculers has not sat," says the psalmist. (Psalm 1:1) Joining in the ridicule in order to deflect the attention from yourself just prolongs the insult cycle. "Return evil for evil to no one. . . . Keep conquering the evil with the good" is godly advice.—Romans 12:17-21.

Ecclesiastes 7:9 further says: "Do not hurry yourself in your spirit to become offended, for the taking of offense is what rests in the bosom of the stupid ones." Yes, why should you take teasing so seriously? Granted, it hurts if someone pokes fun at your physique or finds amusement in your facial blemishes. Nevertheless, the remarks, tasteless though they may be, are not necessarily malicious. So if someone innocently—or even perhaps not so innocently—touches upon some sore spot of yours, why be crushed? If what is said is not obscene or irreverent, try to see the humor in it. There is "a time to laugh," and taking offense at playful teasing may be an overreaction.—Ecclesiastes 3:4.

But what if the teasing is cruel or even vicious? Remember that the ridiculer wants to enjoy your reaction, to revel in your misery. Lashing back, becoming defensive, or bursting into tears is likely to encourage him or her to keep up the harassment. Why give that one the satisfaction of seeing you get upset? The best way to fend off insults is often nonchalantly to ignore them.

King Solomon further said: "Also, do not give your heart to all the words that people may speak ["Don't pay attention to everything people say"—*Today's English Version*], that you may not hear your servant calling down evil upon you. For your own heart well knows even many times that you, even you, have called down evil upon others." (Ecclesiastes 7:21, 22) To "give your heart" to the caustic remarks of the ridiculers would mean to be overly concerned about their judgment of you. Is their judgment valid? The apostle Paul was unfairly attacked by jealous peers, but he replied: "Now to me it is a very trivial matter that I should be examined by you or by a human tribunal. . . . He that examines me is Jehovah." (1 Corinthians 4:3, 4) Paul's relationship with God was so strong that he had the confidence and inward strength to withstand unfair attacks.

Behind the bravado, the tormentors might really be saying: 'We don't like ourselves, but putting someone down makes us feel better'

Letting Your Light Shine

At times you may be mocked because of your way of life as a Christian. Jesus Christ himself had to endure such "contrary talk." (Hebrews 12:3) Jeremiah too "became an object of laughter all day long" because of boldly speaking Jehovah's message. So persistent was the harassment that Jeremiah temporarily lost his incentive. "I am not going to make mention of him [Jehovah], and I shall speak no more in his name," he decided. However, his love for God and truth eventually impelled him to overcome his fear.—Jeremiah 20:7-9.

Some Christian youths today have similarly felt discouraged. Anxious to make the teasing stop, some have tried to conceal the fact that they are Christians. But love for God often finally moves such ones to overcome their fear and to 'let their light shine'! (Matthew 5:16) One teenage boy, for example, said: "My attitude changed. I stopped viewing being a Christian as a burden to carry around and began to view it as something to be proud of." You too can "boast" in the privilege of knowing God and of being used by him to help others.—1 Corinthians 1:31.

Do not, however, invite hostility by constantly criticizing others or by giving others the impression that you feel that you are superior. As opportunity arises to share your

Try displaying a sense of humor when being teased

faith, do so, but with "a mild temper and deep respect." (1 Peter 3:15) Your reputation for fine conduct may prove to be your greatest protection while you are in school. Though others may not like your courageous stand, they will often begrudgingly respect you for it.

A girl named Vanessa was harassed by a group of girls who would hit her, push her around, knock books out of her hands—all in an attempt to provoke a fight. They even poured a chocolate milk shake over her head and clean white dress. Yet she never gave in to the provocation. Sometime later, Vanessa met the group's ringleader at a convention of Jehovah's Witnesses! "I hated you . . . ," the former bully said. "I wanted to see you lose your cool just once." However, her curiosity about how Vanessa maintained her composure led to her accepting a study of the Bible with Jehovah's Witnesses. "I fell in love with what I learned," she continued, "and tomorrow I'm getting baptized."

So do not let "contrary talk" by peers break your spirit. When appropriate, show a sense of humor. Respond to evil with kindness. Refuse to feed the fires of contention, and in time your tormentors may find little pleasure in targeting you for ridicule, for "where there is no wood the fire goes out."—Proverbs 26:20.

Questions for Discussion   Chapter 19

☐ *How does God view those who cruelly tease others?*

☐ *What is often behind youthful harassment?*

☐ *How can you minimize or even halt the ridicule?*

☐ *Why is it important that you "let your light shine" in school, even when others tease you?*

☐ *What steps can you take to protect yourself from violence at school?*

Chapter 20

How Can I Get Along With My Teacher?

"I CAN'T stand an unfair teacher," says young Vicky. No doubt you feel the same way. Yet, in a 1981 survey of 160,000 American youths, 76 percent accused their teachers of some sort of favoritism!

Youths are upset when they get low grades for what they feel is high-grade work. They resent it when discipline seems excessive or uncalled for or seems motivated by racial bias. They are angry when special attention or preferential treatment is given to the teacher's pet.

Granted, teachers are far from infallible. They have their fair share of quirks, problems, and, yes, prejudices. The Bible cautions, however: "Do not hurry yourself in your spirit to become offended." (Ecclesiastes 7:9) Even teachers "stumble many times. If anyone does not stumble in word, this one is a perfect man, able to bridle also his whole body." (James 3:2) Could you therefore give your teacher the benefit of the doubt?

The attention given to teacher's pets often stirs resentment

A youth named Freddy noticed that his teacher "was snapping at everyone." Freddy tactfully approached the teacher and found the cause of this surly behavior. "It's just that I had a problem with my car this morning," the teacher explained. "It overheated on the way to school and I got to work late."

Teachers and Their Pets

What about the special favors accorded to teacher's pets? Bear in mind that a teacher faces unique demands and pressures. The book *Being Adolescent* describes teachers as facing a "serious predicament" in which they must try to hold the attention of a group of youths "whose minds are usually elsewhere . . . They have before them a group of highly moody, distractible teenagers, generally unaccustomed to concentrating on anything for more than 15 minutes."

Is it any wonder, then, that a teacher may lavish attention on the student who studies hard, pays attention, or treats him or her with respect? True, it may gall you when seeming 'apple-polishers' get more attention than you do. But why be upset or jealous if some diligent student is a teacher's pet as long as your educational needs are not ignored? Besides, it may be a good idea to be a bit more diligent yourself.

War in the Classroom

Said one student of his teacher: "He kept thinking that we had all declared war on him and decided to get us first. He was one paranoid person." However, many teachers feel they have a right to be a bit "paranoid." As

the Bible foretold, these are "critical times hard to deal with," and students are often "without self-control, fierce, without love of goodness." (2 Timothy 3:1-3) *U.S. News & World Report* thus said: "Teachers in many urban

159

'My Teacher Is Boring!'

The Family Handbook of Adolescence says: "Some surveys show that the majority of adolescent students are critical of teachers, complaining that they are boring or lacking in humor." Sooner or later you, too, may get a teacher who simply bores you 'to tears.' What can you do?

One recent experiment revealed that a teenager's level of concentration is quite high in classes such as the industrial arts, physical education, and music. However, the level of concentration nose-dives in classes dealing with language and history.

Are physical-education or music instructors more gifted than teachers of academic subjects? Not likely. Evidently, many students simply have a negative attitude toward academic subjects. And if students decide in advance that a subject is boring, even a teacher with the skills of Socrates would have a hard time holding their attention! Could it be, then, that your attitude toward certain subjects simply needs adjusting? Taking more of an interest in what you learn may take the boredom out of school.

At times even students interested in learning complain that they have "bad" teachers. But just what is a "good" teacher? Said one young girl: "I like my math teacher because she's a lot of fun." One boy praised his English teacher for 'cracking a lot of jokes.'

But while being likable or even entertaining can be an asset for a teacher, it is not a substitute for his being "adequately qualified to teach others." (2 Timothy 2:2) Though the Bible refers here to spiritual qualifications, it highlights the fact that a good teacher should know his subject.

Unfortunately, knowledge and a colorful personality do not always come in the same package. The apostle Paul, for example,

er. Try taking notes in order to keep your attention riveted on what he has to say. Supplement dull classroom discussions with additional study at home.

Barbara Mayer, a teacher herself, adds: "Teachers, who have probably repeated these same lessons more times than they care to remember, tend to fall into a routine." What can you do to liven things up? "Raise your hand for a change and ask for more information . . . Make him really tell you all he knows." Will the teacher resent this? Not if you do so respectfully. (Colossians 4:6) Says Mayer: "You'll discover that your teacher is coming to class a bit more prepared, and with more than just surface information."

Enthusiasm is contagious, and your desire to learn just might inject some life into your teacher. Of course, don't expect a drastic transformation. And there may be some classes that you just have to suffer through. But if you are a good listener and are sincerely interested in what is going on, you can still learn —even from a boring teacher.

was superbly qualified as an instructor of God's Word. Yet some Christians in Paul's day complained that "his presence in person [was] weak and his speech contemptible." Paul replied: "Even if I am unskilled in speech, I certainly am not in knowledge." (2 Corinthians 10:10; 11:6) If some overlooked what Paul had to say and saw only his alleged deficiencies as a speaker, they lost out on gaining valuable knowledge. Don't make the same mistake when it comes to school! Before writing off a teacher as being "bad," ask yourself, 'Does he know what he is talking about? Can I learn from him?'

You may have to pay more than the usual attention to the teacher who is a drab speak-

The rising tide of school violence has made the teacher's job a difficult one

school districts live with the fear of violence."

Former teacher Roland Betts says concerning teachers: "Children see it as their inherent responsibility to . . . [figuratively] push them and poke them and see just how far they will bend or stretch before they will finally snap . . . When the children sense that they have pushed a new teacher to within a hair's breadth of his breaking point, they push some more." Have you or your classmates been party to teacher harassment? Then don't be surprised at your teacher's reaction.

The Bible says: "Mere oppression may make a wise one act crazy." (Ecclesiastes 7:7) In the atmosphere of fear and disrespect that pervades certain schools, some teachers understandably overreact and become harsh disciplinarians. Observes *The Family Handbook of Adolescence:* "Students who . . . seem by their behavior to belittle teachers' beliefs are usually belittled in return." Yes, the hostile teacher is often molded by his students!

Also, consider the effects of cruel classroom pranks. Young Valerie exaggerates little when she speaks of "the torture, the torment," youngsters put substitute teachers through. Adds Roland Betts: "Substitutes are hounded unmercifully by their classes, often pushed to the point of cracking and breaking." Certain that they can get away with it, students delight in having sudden

162   *YOUNG PEOPLE ASK . . .*

attacks of clumsiness—dropping their books or pencils on the floor in unison. Or they may try to frustrate their teacher by 'playing dumb' and acting as if they cannot understand a word he says. "We sabotage for fun," explains young Bobby.

Nevertheless, if you sow classroom cruelty, don't be surprised if you reap a mean, hostile teacher. (Compare Galatians 6:7.) Remember the golden rule: "All things, therefore, that you want men to do to you, you also must likewise do to them." (Matthew 7:12) Refuse to join in classroom pranks. Be attentive to what your teacher says. Be cooperative. Perhaps in time he will feel a little less hostile—at least toward you.

'My Teacher Doesn't Like Me'

At times a clash of personalities or some sort of misunderstanding sets your teacher against you; inquisitiveness is confused with rebellion or a touch of whimsy with foolishness. And if a teacher dislikes you, he may be inclined to embarrass or humiliate you. Mutual animosity may flourish.

> "*Teachers in many urban school districts live with the fear of violence.*" —*U.S.News & World Report*

The Bible says: "Return evil for evil to no one. . . . If possible, as far as it depends upon you, be peaceable with all men." (Romans 12:17, 18) Try not to antagonize your teacher. Avoid needless confrontations. Give your teacher no legitimate cause for complaint. In fact, try to be friendly. 'Friendly? To *him?*' you ask. Yes, show manners by respectfully greeting your teacher when you come to class. Your persistent politeness—even a smile from time to time—just might change his opinion of you.—Compare Romans 12:20, 21.

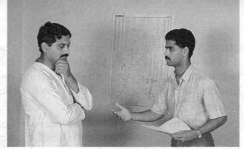

If you feel some injustice has occurred, respectfully approach your teacher

True, you cannot always smile your way out of a situation. But Ecclesiastes 10:4 does advise: "If the spirit of a ruler [or person in authority] should mount up against you [by chastising you], do not leave your own place, for calmness itself allays great sins." Remember, too, that "an answer, when mild, turns away rage."—Proverbs 15:1.

'I Deserved a Better Grade'

This is a common complaint. Try talking out the problem with your teacher. The Bible tells of how Nathan approached the difficult task of exposing a serious shortcoming on the part of King David. Nathan did not barge into the palace shouting accusations, but he approached David tactfully.—2 Samuel 12:1-7.

You might likewise humbly, and *calmly,* approach your teacher. Former schoolteacher Bruce Weber reminds us: "Rebellion in a student provokes obstinacy in a teacher. If you rant and rave or claim gross injustice and vow revenge, you'll get nowhere." Try a more adult approach. Maybe you can begin by asking your teacher to help you understand his grading system. Then, says Weber, you can "try to prove yourself the victim of an oversight or miscalculation rather than of bad judgment. Use your teacher's own grading system; show her where you see the error in your grade." Even if your grade is not changed, your maturity will probably make a positive impression upon your teacher.

Let Your Parents Know

At times, though, mere talk proves fruitless. Take Susan's experience. As an honor student, she was shocked when one of her teachers started giving her failing grades. The problem? Susan was one of Jehovah's Witnesses, and her teacher as much as admitted that she disliked Susan because of this. "It was really frustrating," says Susan, "and I didn't know what to do."

Recalls Susan: "I gathered up courage and told my mother [a single parent] about this teacher. She said, 'Well, maybe I can talk to your teacher.' And during open house she went up and asked my teacher what the problem was. I thought my mother was really going to get upset, but she didn't. She just calmly talked to her." The teacher arranged for Susan to have a different teacher.

Admittedly, not all tangled affairs have neat endings, and at times you just have to endure. But if you can coexist peaceably with your teacher this term, there is always next year, when you'll have a fresh start, perhaps different classmates—and perhaps even a new teacher to learn to get along with.

Questions for Discussion   *Chapter 20*

☐ *How can you view a teacher who treats you unfairly?*

☐ *Why do teachers often heap attention on so-called pets?*

☐ *How can you learn from a teacher who seems boring?*

☐ *Why do some teachers seem hostile toward their students?*

☐ *How can you apply the golden rule in the classroom?*

☐ *What can you do if you feel you are a victim of unfair grading or treatment?*

Chapter 21

How Can I Get (and Keep!) a Job?

A SURVEY, published in *Senior Scholastic* magazine, asked some American high school seniors to rate which life goals they considered "very important." Eighty-four percent responded: "Being able to find steady work."

Perhaps you are interested in an afterschool job to help out with personal or household expenses. Or you may be seeking part-time employment in order to support yourself as a full-time evangelizer. (See Chapter 22.) In any event, worldwide inflation and limited demand for unskilled workers have made jobs hard to come by if you are a youth. How, then, can you make a smooth entry into the job market?

School—A Job-Training Ground

Cleveland Jones, an employment recruiter with many years of experience, offers this advice: "Get a good high school education. I cannot stress enough the importance of learning to read and write and speak properly. Learn proper decorum as well, so you can handle people in the working world."

"I cannot stress enough the importance of learning to read and write and speak properly"

A bus driver must be able to read timetables for arrivals and departures. Factory workers need to know how to fill out job-completion tickets or similar reports. Salesclerks are expected to do computations. In almost every type of job, communication skills are needed. These are skills you can master in school.

Persistence Pays Off

"Never give up if you are out of school and looking for a job," says Jones. "Do not go out on two or three interviews, then go home and sit and wait. You will never get called for a job that way." Young Sal looked for a job for seven months before he was hired. "I would tell myself: 'My job is to find a job,'" explains Sal. "I would spend eight hours a day each weekday for seven months looking for a job. I would start early each morning and 'work' till four o'clock in the afternoon. Many nights my feet would be sore. The next morning I would have to 'psych myself up' to start looking again."

What kept Sal from quitting? "Every time I was in a personnel office," he answers, "I would remember what Jesus said: 'Exert yourselves vigorously.' I would keep thinking that one day I will be working and that this bad time would pass."—Luke 13:24.

The skills you learn in school may one day prove valuable on a job

Handling Job Interviews

*"**Before going** on a job interview, remember, first impressions are lasting impressions,"* advises job counselor Cleveland Jones. He cautions against wearing jeans and sneakers to an interview and stresses the need to be clean and neat. Employers often conclude that the way a person dresses is the way the person will work.

When applying for an office job, dress as a business person dresses. When applying for a factory job, wear slacks and a shirt that are clean and pressed, along with neat-looking shoes. If you are a woman, dress modestly and use cosmetics sparingly. And if applying for an office job, wear hose and dress shoes to complement a conservative outfit.

Always go alone to a job interview, cautions Jones. If you bring your mother or friends with you to the interview, the employer may conclude that you are immature.

'**Suppose** the employer asks me if I have had prior work experience, how do I answer?' you may wonder. Do not bluff. Employers often see through exaggeration. Be honest.

You may not realize it, but you have likely had prior work experience even if you are hunting for your first "real" job. Did you ever have a summer

Where to Find Jobs

If you live in a rural area, your job search could start with local farms and orchards, or you can look for some type of yard work. If you live in a large town or city, try looking in the newspaper help-wanted ads. These ads give clues as to what qualifications are needed for a certain job and can help you to explain to the employer why you can fill those needs. Parents, teachers, employment agencies, personnel offices, friends, and neighbors are other sources you can tap.

job? Or did you ever baby-sit? Did you have a regular work assignment in your home caring for family chores? Were you given the responsibility to take care of certain duties at your place of worship? Have you ever had training in public speaking? If so, then these things could be mentioned at the interview or listed in your résumé to show that you can handle responsibility.

Another important concern of employers is how interested you are in their company and the job being offered. You must convince them that you want to do the work and can do it. The "what's-in-it-for-me" attitude will quickly turn off the interviewer's interest in you.

Applying for and getting a full- or part-time job is a challenge that you can meet successfully. And when that job is used as a tool to help others, not just yourself, satisfaction becomes a fringe benefit.

Keeping Your Job

Unfortunately, when economic pressures create unemployment, employed youths are usually among the first to be fired. But this need not happen to you. "People who retain jobs are people who are willing to work and who show a willing attitude to do whatever the employer asks," says Mr. Jones.

Your attitude is your state of mind—how you feel about your job as well as the people you work for and work with. Your attitude will be reflected in the quality of work you do. Your boss will judge your worth on the basis of not only your work output but also your attitude.

"Let your employer see that not only can you follow instructions but you can do more than what is required without constant supervision," continues Jones. "Because in a tight labor market, the workers who remain are not necessarily those who have been there the longest, but those who produce."

Sal found this to be true. He says: "I always tried to accommodate my employer. I was willing to bend my schedule when necessary, follow instructions and be respectful to my supervisors." This reminds one of the Bible's exhortation "to obey your human masters, not with the idea of catching their eye or currying favour, but as a sincere expression of your devotion to the Lord."—Colossians 3:22, *Phillips.*

Overcoming Fear

If you are new on the job, fear is a common emotion for the first few days. You may wonder: 'Will they like me? Can I do the job? Will they like my work? I hope I will not look stupid.' Here you need to be careful, or your fears will nibble away at your positive outlook.

"I would tell myself: 'My job is to find a job'"

You can quicken your adjustment and calm your nerves by learning more about the company. Look, listen, and read. *At the proper time* ask your supervisor reasonable questions about your job and your performance—it will not make you look foolish. Ask yourself, 'How does my job fit in with my department, with the overall company objective?' The answers can help you to develop good work habits and job satisfaction.

170

What to Do During the Job Interview

Be grown-up, businesslike. Greet employer with proper respect. Call him "Mr."—not "Jack," "Buddy," or "Pal."

Sit up straight in chair, feet firmly on floor; look alert. Advance planning will help you to be calm, poised, and at ease.

Think before answering a question. Be polite, accurate, honest, and frank. Give full information. Do not brag.

Have a guide sheet with you, listing all your jobs, dates of work, wages, kinds of work you did, reasons you left.

Be ready to show how your training and work experience will help you to get ahead on job you are asking for.

For references, give the names (and complete addresses) of three reliable people who know you and your work.

Be confident, enthusiastic, but do not bluff. Use good English and speak distinctly. Do not talk too much.

Listen carefully; be polite and tactful. Above all, do not get into any arguments with your prospective employer.

The employer is interested only in how well you will fit the job. Do not mention personal, home, or money problems.

If it seems you will not get the job, seek employer's advice about other jobs that may come up with the firm.

Send employer brief thank-you letter immediately after interview.*

---

* Source: New York State Employment Service Office brochure *How to "Sell Yourself" to an Employer.*

Get Along With Coworkers

All jobs ultimately involve dealing with other people. Knowing how to maintain good relations with others is thus essential to keeping a job. "If possible, as far as it depends upon you, be peaceable with all men." (Romans 12:18) Doing so can help you avoid needless bickering or heated confrontations on the job.

Sometimes the people you work with have backgrounds and personalities quite different from yours. But do not think that someone is inferior because he is different. Respect his right to be different. No person likes to be treated with lack of respect; it makes him feel as if he is a nobody. Everyone likes to feel he is wanted and needed—a somebody. Win the respect of your fellow employees and employer by treating them with respect.

Avoiding Gossip

"It's a bad pitfall," says Sal, "because gossip could give you a poor impression of the boss or others." The grapevine is not the best source of information, and it may result in sour grapes for you. The rumors growing on the grapevine are usually gross exaggerations that can damage the reputation of others—as well as your own reputation. Therefore, smother the urge to gossip.

Remember, too, that no one likes a complainer. If something is bothering you on the job, don't broadcast it through the grapevine. Go and talk to your supervisor. Do not, however, burst into his office in a heat of rage and be sorry later for rash words. Also, avoid the snare of personal attacks. Keep to the facts. Be as clear and honest as you can be in describing the problem. Maybe you could begin with an opening statement such as, 'I need your help . . . ' or, 'I may be wrong, but I feel this way about . . . '

Punctuality Is Important

Two big reasons why people fail to keep a job are being late for work and missing days from work. An employment and training director for a large industrial city said about young workers: "They need to learn to get up in the morning, to learn how to take orders. If they never learn these things, it just perpetuates the unemployment syndrome."

Sal learned the lesson of punctuality the hard way. "I lost my first job after just three months because of tardiness," he sighs, "and this made it more difficult to find other jobs."

The Value of Honesty

Says employment recruiter Jones: "Honesty will help a person keep the job." Being honest includes avoiding not only the stealing of material things but also the stealing of time by taking excessive breaks. An honest employee is valued and trusted. For example, one young witness of Jehovah who worked at an exclusive clothing store had a reputation for honesty.

"One day," he recalls, "the manager found an item in the stockroom, hidden inside some other clothing. One of the workers was stealing from the store. At closing time I went upstairs to the manager's office and to my surprise all the employees were there. All the employees were kept there to be searched. I was the *only* employee excused from the search."

Many Christian youths have had similar experiences and have become valued employees. Work hard, then, at finding work. Be persistent. Do not give up. And when you find that job you've looked for so hard, work hard to keep it!

Questions for Discussion   *Chapter 21*

☐ *How can your schoolwork affect your ability to find a job?*

☐ *Why is it important to be persistent when job hunting?*

☐ *What are some places to look and people to consult when seeking employment?*

☐ *What are some tips for handling a job interview?*

☐ *What can you do to protect yourself from being fired?*

Chapter 22

What Career Should I Choose?

'WHAT shall I do with the rest of my life?' Sooner or later you confront this challenging question. A confusing array of choices present themselves—medicine, business, art, education, computer science, engineering, the trades. And you may feel like the youth who said: "What I consider to be successful . . . is maintaining the comfort level that you grew up with." Or like others, you may dream of improving your financial lot in life.

But is there more to success than material gain? Can any secular career bring you real fulfillment?

'It Didn't Mean a Thing'

Glamorous, exciting, lucrative! That is the way movies, TV, and books often portray secular careers. But to attain so-called success, career climbers must often vie with one another in a life-and-death struggle for recognition. Dr. Douglas LaBier tells of how young adults, many "with fast-track, hi-tech careers, report feelings of dissatisfaction, anxiety, depression, emptiness, paranoia, as well as a whole range of physical complaints."

Long ago, King Solomon exposed the futility of mere worldly success. Backed by virtually limitless resources, Solomon built up an astonishing list of career accomplishments. (Read Ecclesiastes 2:4-10.) Yet, concluded Solomon: "I, even I, turned toward all the works of mine that my hands had done and toward the hard work that I had worked hard to accomplish, and, look! everything was vanity ["I realized that it didn't mean a

174   *YOUNG PEOPLE ASK . . .*

thing," *Today's English Version*] and a striving after wind."—Ecclesiastes 2:11.

A job may well bring wealth and recognition, but it cannot satisfy one's 'spiritual needs.' (Matthew 5:3) Satisfaction thus eludes those who build their lives solely around secular achievement.

A Career That Satisfies

King Solomon advises: "The conclusion of the matter, everything having been heard, is: Fear the true God and keep his commandments. For this is the whole obligation of man." (Ecclesiastes 12:13) The prime obligation for Christians today is to preach the Kingdom message. (Matthew 24:14) *A job may well bring wealth and recognition, but it cannot satisfy one's 'spiritual needs'* And youths who take seriously their obligation before God feel compelled to have as full a share in this work as possible—even if they are not naturally inclined toward preaching. (Compare 2 Corinthians 5:14.) Instead of pursuing full-time secular jobs, thousands have chosen to serve as full-time pioneer evangelizers. Others serve as foreign missionaries or at branch offices of the Watch Tower Society.

Emily, who gave up a career as an executive secretary to become a pioneer, says: "I have developed a real love for this work." Yes, the full-time ministry is the most satisfying, exciting career imaginable! And what greater privilege could one have than to be one of "God's fellow workers"?—1 Corinthians 3:9.

University Education—Advantageous?

Most pioneer ministers support themselves with part-time work. But what if later on you need to support a family? Surely one would never regret devoting one's youthful years to God's service! Still, would it not make sense for a youth first to obtain a university degree and perhaps pursue the ministry later?

The Bible, of course, does not spell out exactly how many years of schooling a Christian youth should obtain. Nor does it condemn education. Jehovah, the "Grand Instructor," encourages his people to read well and to express themselves clearly. (Isaiah 30:20; Psalm 1:2; Hebrews 5:12) Moreover, education can broaden our understanding of people and the world we live in.

Nevertheless, is a university degree always worth the huge commitment of time and money it demands?* While statistics indicate that university graduates earn higher salaries and suffer less unemployment than high school graduates, the book *Planning Your College Education* reminds us that these statistics are mere averages. Only a minority of university graduates actually receive sky-high salaries; the rest are paid wages that are far more down to earth. Besides, the high incomes attributed to university graduates may also result from such factors as "unusual abilities, motivation, area opportunities for employment, . . . special talents"—not simply the amount of their education.

"A [university] degree no longer guarantees success in the job market," says the U.S. Department of Labor. "The proportion [of university graduates] employed in professional, technical, and managerial occupations . . . declined because these occupations did not expand rapidly enough to absorb the growing supply of graduates. As a result, roughly 1 out of 5 [university] graduates who entered the labor market between 1970 and 1984 took a job not usually requiring a degree. This oversupply of graduates is likely to continue through the mid-1990's."

---

* In the United States, university costs average well over $10,000 a year! It often takes students years to pay off their indebtedness.

YOUNG PEOPLE ASK . . .

Further Facts to Ponder

A university degree may or may not improve your employment prospects. But one fact is indisputable: "The time left is reduced"! (1 Corinthians 7:29) For all its presumed benefits, would four years or more in a university be the best use of that remaining time?—Ephesians 5:16.

> **"A [university] degree no longer guarantees success in the job market"**

Would a university education steer you toward or away from your spiritual goals? Remember, a high income is not a Christian priority. (1 Timothy 6:7, 8) Yet, a survey of U.S. university administrators described today's students as 'career-oriented, concerned with material success, concerned with self.' One group of students said: "Money. It seems like all we talk about is money." How might being immersed in an atmosphere of intense competition and selfish materialism affect you?

Universities may no longer have the riotous scenes of the 1960's. But a decrease in university bedlam hardly means the campus environment is wholesome. Concluded one study of campus life: "Students still have almost unlimited freedom in personal and social matters." Drugs and alcohol are used freely, and promiscuity is the rule—not the exception. If this is true of universities in your land, might living there thwart your efforts to remain morally clean?—1 Corinthians 6:18.

Another concern is the well-documented association of exposure to higher education with decreased "adherence to core religious tenets." (*The Sacred in a Secular Age*) The pressure to maintain high grades has caused some Christian youths to neglect spiritual activities and thus become vulnerable to the onslaught of secular thinking promoted by universities. Some have suffered shipwreck concerning their faith.—Colossians 2:8.

Alternatives to University Education

In view of these facts, many Christian youths have decided against a university education. Many have found that the training offered in congregations of Jehovah's Witnesses—the weekly Theocratic Ministry School in particular—has given them a real edge in finding employment. Though not possessing a university degree, such youths learn to be poised, adept at expressing themselves, and quite capable of handling responsibility. Furthermore, while in secondary school, some take courses in typing, computer programming, auto repair, machine-shop work, and so forth. Such skills may lend themselves to part-time employment and are often in high demand. And though many youths disdain 'working with their hands,' the Bible dignifies doing "hard work." (Ephesians 4:28; compare Proverbs 22:29.) Why, Jesus Christ himself learned a trade so well that he came to be called "the carpenter"!—Mark 6:3.

True, in some lands university graduates have so flooded the job market that it is hard to obtain even commonplace jobs without some additional job training. But often there are apprenticeship programs, vocational or technical schools, and short-term university courses that teach marketable skills with a minimum investment of time and money. Never forget, too, that there is a factor that employment statistics do not take into account: God's promise to provide for those who give priority to spiritual interests.—Matthew 6:33.

Employment prospects and educational systems vary from place to place. Youths have different abilities and inclinations. And while a career in the Christian ministry is recommended as being beneficial, it is still a matter of personal choice. You and your parents must thus carefully weigh all factors involved in deciding how much education is right for you. 'Each one must carry his own load' in making such decisions.—Galatians 6:5.

If, for example, your parents insist that you attend a university, you have no choice but to obey them as long as you are living under their supervision.* (Ephesians 6: 1-3) Perhaps you can continue living at home and avoid getting caught up in the university scene. Be selective in your choice of courses, for example, focusing on learning job skills rather than worldly philosophies. Guard your associations. (1 Corinthians 15:33) Keep yourself spiritually strong by meeting attendance, field service, and personal study. Some youths who have been obliged to attend university have even managed to pioneer by choosing a schedule of courses that made that possible.

Choose your career carefully and prayerfully, so that it not only will bring personal happiness but will enable you to 'store up treasures in heaven.'—Matthew 6:20.

---

* It may not be necessary to receive a four-year degree to satisfy your parents. In the United States, an associate degree, for example, is acceptable to employers in many professional and service-related fields and can be acquired in two years.

Questions for Discussion   Chapter 22

☐ *Why do secular careers often fail to bring personal happiness?*

☐ *Why should all God-fearing youths consider a career in the full-time ministry?*

☐ *What are the claimed benefits of higher education, and do such claims always hold true?*

☐ *What dangers might university education pose?*

☐ *What alternatives to university education can a youth consider?*

Sex and Morals

*M*any youths will no doubt turn to this section of the book first. Why? Because no subject generates as many questions and as much controversy—and confusion—as sex and morals. Morality, however, encompasses more than sexual behavior. For example, can you call a youth moral who lies and cheats? Or are there situations in which dishonesty is OK? Fortunately, the Bible gives us some direct and practical guidelines on these matters of morality.

Chapter 23

What About Sex Before Marriage?

'IF YOU love each other, is it all right? Or should you wait until you're married?' 'I'm still a virgin. Is there something wrong with me?' Questions like these abound among youths.

Nevertheless, "It is the exceptional young person who has not had sexual intercourse while still a teenager," concluded the Alan Guttmacher Institute in its 1981 report. "Eight in 10 males and seven in 10 females report having had intercourse while in their teens."

'And why not?' you may ask. After all, it is only natural to want to feel loved. And when you're young, your passions can be powerful to the point of distraction. Furthermore, there's the influence of your peers. They may tell you that premarital sex is fun and that when you really like someone, it's only natural to want to be intimate. Some may even say that having sex proves your manhood or womanhood. Not wanting to be viewed as odd, you may thus feel under pressure to experience sexual relations.

Contrary to popular opinion, not all youths are in a hurry to give up their virginity. Consider, for example, a young single woman named Esther. She was getting a medical checkup when her doctor matter-of-factly inquired: "What method of contraception are you using?" When Esther replied, "I'm not using any," her doctor exclaimed: "What! Do you want to get pregnant? How do you expect not to get pregnant if you're not using anything?" Esther replied: "Because I'm not having sex!"

Her doctor stared at her in disbelief. "This is unbelievable," he said. "Kids come in here 13 years old, and they are no longer virgins. You are a remarkable person."

> "It is the exceptional young person who has not had sexual intercourse while still a teenager."—The Alan Guttmacher Institute

What made Esther "remarkable"? She obeyed the Bible's admonition: "Now the body is not for fornication [including premarital sex] . . . Flee from fornication." (1 Corinthians 6: 13, 18) Yes, she recognized premarital sex as a serious sin against God! "This is what God wills," states 1 Thessalonians 4:3, "that you abstain from fornication." Why, though, does the Bible forbid premarital sex?

The Aftereffects

Even in Bible times, some engaged in premarital sex. An immoral woman might invite a young man to indulge, saying: "Do come, let us drink our fill of love until the morning; do let us enjoy each other with love expressions." (Proverbs 7:18) The Bible, however, warned that pleasures enjoyed today can cause pain tomorrow. "For as a honeycomb the lips of a strange woman keep dripping, and her palate is smoother than oil," observed Solomon. "But," he continued, "the aftereffect from her is as bitter as wormwood; it is as sharp as a two-edged sword."—Proverbs 5:3, 4.

One possible aftereffect is the contracting of a sexually transmitted disease. Imagine the heartache if years later one learned that a sexual experience has caused irreversible damage, perhaps infertility or a serious health problem! As Proverbs 5:11 warns: "You have to groan in your future when your flesh and your organism come to an end." Premarital sex also leads to illegitimacy (see pages 184-5), abortion, and premature marriage —each with its painful consequences. Yes, one engaging in premarital sex truly 'sins against his or her own body.'—1 Corinthians 6:18.

Recognizing such dangers, Dr. Richard Lee wrote in the *Yale Journal of Biology and Medicine:* "We boast to our young people about our great breakthroughs in preventing pregnancy and treating venereal disease disregarding the most reliable and specific, the least expensive and toxic, preventative of both gestational and venereal distress—the ancient, honorable, and even healthy state of virginity."

Guilt and Disappointment

Many youths have further found premarital sex to be bitterly disappointing. The result? Feelings of guilt and diminished self-respect. Twenty-three-year-old Dennis admitted: "It was a big letdown—no feeling of good or warmth of love as it was supposed to be. Rather the full realization of how wrong the act was hit me. I felt totally ashamed at my lack of self-control." Confessed a young woman: "I came back to reality with a sickening

In the wake of immoral sex, a youth often feels exploited or even humiliated

'It Can't Happen to Me!'
—The Problem of Teen Pregnancy

"More than one in 10 teenagers gets pregnant each year, and the proportion is rising. If patterns do not change, four in 10 young women will get pregnant at least once while still in their teens." So reports Teenage Pregnancy: The Problem That Hasn't Gone Away. And what kind of girls get pregnant? Said the journal Adolescence: "School-age girls who become pregnant come from all socioeconomic classes . . . All races, all faiths, and all parts of the country, rural and urban."*

Few girls actually want to become pregnant. In his landmark study of over 400 pregnant teenagers, Frank Furstenberg, Jr., observed that "most remarked repeatedly in the interviews, 'I never thought it would happen to me.'"

But observing that some of their friends had enjoyed sexual relations without getting pregnant, some girls figured they could do so, too. Furstenberg also states: "A number mentioned that they did not think it was possible to become pregnant 'right away.' Others thought that if they had sexual relations only 'every once in a while' they would not become pregnant . . . The longer they went without conceiving, the

more likely they were to assume greater risks."

The truth is, however, that whenever one engages in sexual relations there is the risk of pregnancy. (Of one group of 544 girls, 'nearly one-fifth became pregnant within six months after beginning sexual intercourse.') Many, like an unwed mother named Robin, deliberately choose not to utilize birth control. Robin feared —as do many youths—that using the birth-control pill would damage her health. She further admits: "For me to obtain birth control, I would have had to admit to myself that I was doing something wrong. I couldn't do that. So I just blocked what I was doing out

of my mind and hoped nothing would happen."

Such reasoning is common among unwed mothers. In Furstenberg's study, "nearly half of the teenagers stated that it was very important for a woman to wait until marriage to begin to have sex . . . Undeniably, there was an obvious discrepancy between the words and the deeds . . . They had acquired one set of standards and had learned to live by another." This emotional conflict "made it especially difficult for these women to deal realistically with the consequences of their sexual behavior."

Even using birth control is no guarantee that a girl will escape unwed motherhood. The book <u>Kids</u> <u>Having</u> <u>Kids</u> reminds us: "Every method has a failure

rate. . . . Even if unmarried teens consistently use birth control methods . . . 500,000 [in the U.S.] would still become pregnant each year." A 16-year-old unwed mother named Pat is then quoted as lamenting: "I took [birth-control pills] faithfully. I honestly never missed a day."

"Do not be misled," warns the Bible. "God is not one to be mocked. For whatever a man is sowing, this he will also reap." (Galatians 6:7) Pregnancy is just one of the ways one can reap an unpleasant harvest from fornication. Fortunately, unwed mothers, like all others who have become entrapped in immorality, can turn around and come to God with the repentant attitude of King David, who prayed: "Thoroughly wash me from my error, and cleanse me even from my sin." (Psalm 51:2) God will bless the efforts of such repentant ones to raise their children "in the discipline and mental-regulating of Jehovah." —Ephesians 6:4.

Better it is, though, to avoid premarital sex! Do not be fooled by those who say you can get away with it.

thud. . . . The party was over and I felt sick, cheap, and dirty. It didn't make me feel any better to hear him say, 'Why on earth didn't you stop us before things went too far?'"

Such reactions are not rare, according to Dr. Jay Segal. After studying the sexual activities of 2,436 college students, he concluded: "Dissatisfying and disappointing first [sexual intercourse] experiences exceeded those that were fulfilling and exciting by a ratio of almost two to one. Both males and females recalled that they were greatly disappointed." Granted, even married couples may sometimes have their difficulties when it comes to sex. But in a marriage, where there is genuine love and commitment, such problems usually can be worked out.

The Price of Promiscuity

Some youths feel no guilt whatsoever about having relations, and so they go all out for sensual gratification, seeking sex with a variety of partners. Researcher Robert Sorensen, in his study of teenage sexuality, observed that such youths pay a price for their promiscuity. Writes Sorensen: "In our personal interviews, many [promiscuous youths] reveal . . . that they believe they are functioning with little purpose and self-

Sexually transmitted diseases often result from premarital sex

contentment." Forty-six percent of these agreed with the statement, "The way I'm living right now, most of my abilities are going to waste." Sorensen further found that these promiscuous youths reported low "self-confidence and self-esteem."

It is just as Proverbs 5:9 says: Those engaging in immorality "give to others [their] dignity."

The Morning After

Once a couple have had illicit relations, they often look at each other differently. A boy may find that his feelings for the girl are not as intense as before; he may even find her less attractive. A girl, on the other hand, may feel

> *"It was a big letdown—no feeling of good or warmth of love as it was supposed to be"*

exploited. Recall the Bible account of the young man Amnon and how lovesick he was over the virgin Tamar. Yet, after intercourse with her, "Amnon began hating her with a very great hatred."—2 Samuel 13:15.

A girl named Maria had a similar experience. After having sexual relations, she admitted: "I hated myself (for my weakness), and I hated my boyfriend. In fact, the sex relations we thought would bring us closer ended our relationship. I didn't even want to see him again." Yes, by having premarital sex, a couple cross a line over which they can never go back!

Paul H. Landis, a respected researcher in the field of family life, observes: "The temporary effect [of premarital sex] may be to strengthen the relationship, but the long-term effects may be quite different." Indeed, couples who have sex are more likely to break up than are those who abstain! The reason? Illicit sex breeds jealousy and distrust. Admitted one youth: "Some fellows, when they have intercourse, think afterwards, 'if she had it with me maybe she had it with someone else.' As a matter of fact, I felt that way. . . . I was extremely jealous and doubtful, and suspicious."

How remote this is from genuine love, which "is not jealous, . . . does not behave indecently, does not look for its own interests." (1 Corinthians 13:4, 5) The love that builds lasting relationships is not based on blind passion.

The Benefits of Chastity—Peace and Self-Respect

Staying chaste, however, does more than help a youth avoid dire consequences. The Bible tells of a young maiden who remained chaste despite intense love for her boyfriend. As a result, she could proudly say: "I am a wall, and my breasts are like towers." She was no 'swinging door' that easily 'opened up' under immoral pressure. Morally, she stood like the unscalable wall of a fortress with inaccessible towers! She deserved to be called "the pure one" and could say of her prospective husband, "I have become in his eyes like her that is finding peace." Her own peace of mind contributed to the contentment between the two of them.—Song of Solomon 6:9, 10; 8:9, 10.

Esther, the chaste girl mentioned previously, had the same inner peace and self-esteem. She said: "I felt

Excessive displays of affection can expose a couple to moral dangers and curtail meaningful communication

Marital happiness depends upon more than a couple's physical relationship

good about myself. Even when workmates would ridicule me, I viewed my virginity like a diamond, valuable because it is so rare." Additionally, youths like Esther are not plagued by a guilty conscience. "There is nothing nicer than to have a good conscience toward Jehovah God," stated Stefan, a 19-year-old Christian.

'But how can a couple get to know each other well if they don't have sex?' wonder some youths.

Building Lasting Intimacy

Sex alone cannot forge a permanent relationship; neither can expressions of affection, such as kissing. A young woman named Ann warns: "I learned from experience that at times you can get too close physically too soon." When a couple spend their time lavishing affection upon each other, meaningful communication ceases. They may thus gloss over serious differences that can resurface after marriage. When Ann later began to date another man—the one she eventually married—she was careful to avoid becoming too intimate physically. Explains Ann: "We spent our time working out problems and discussing our goals in life. I got to know what type of *person* I was marrying. After marriage, there were only pleasant surprises."

Was it hard for Ann and her boyfriend to show such self-control? "Yes, it was!" confessed Ann. "I am just naturally an affectionate person. But we talked about the dangers and helped each other. We both wanted very much to please God and not spoil our upcoming marriage."

But does it not help for a new husband or wife to have previous sexual experience? No, on the contrary, it often detracts from marital intimacy! In premarital relations, the emphasis is on self-gratification, the physical aspects of sex. Mutual respect is undermined by uncontrolled passion. Once such selfish patterns are formed, they are hard to break and can eventually wreak havoc on the relationship.

> *By having premarital sex, a couple cross a line over which they can never go back!*

In marriage, however, a healthy intimate relationship demands restraint, self-control. The focus must be on giving, *'rendering* one's sexual due,' rather than *getting.* (1 Corinthians 7:3, 4) Staying chaste helps you develop such self-control. It teaches you to put unselfish concern for the other's welfare ahead of your own desires. Remember, too, that marital satisfaction is not purely due to physical factors. Sociologist Seymour Fisher says that a woman's sexual response also depends upon her having "feelings of intimacy, closeness, and dependability" and upon her husband's "ability to identify with his wife, and . . . how much confidence she had in him."

Interestingly, in a study of 177 married women, three fourths of those who had engaged in premarital sex reported sexual difficulties during the first two weeks of marriage. Furthermore, all who reported long-term sexual difficulties "had histories of premarital intercourse." Research has further shown that those engaging in premarital sex are twice as likely to commit adultery after marriage! How true are the Bible's words: "Fornication . . . take[s] away good motive."—Hosea 4:11.

Therefore, 'you will reap what you sow.' (Galatians 6:7, 8) Sow passion and reap a bumper crop of doubts and insecurities. But if you sow self-control, you will reap a harvest of fidelity and security. Esther, mentioned earlier, has since been happily married for several years now. Says her husband, "It's an indescribable joy to come home to my wife and know that we belong only to each other. Nothing can replace this feeling of confidence."

Those who wait until marriage also enjoy peace of mind, knowing they are pleasing to God. Still, staying chaste these days is far from easy. What can help you to do so?

Questions for Discussion   *Chapter 23*

□ *How prevalent is premarital sex among the youths you know? Does this create any problems or pressures for you?*

□ *What are some of the negative aftereffects of premarital sex? Do you know of any youths who have suffered in these ways?*

□ *Is birth control the answer to the problem of teen pregnancy?*

□ *Why do some feel guilt and disappointment after engaging in illicit sex?*

□ *Do you feel that sexual relations will help an unmarried couple to draw closer to each other? Why do you so answer?*

□ *How can a couple get to know each other while dating?*

□ *What do you think are the benefits of remaining virgin until marriage?*

Chapter 24

How Can I Say No to Premarital Sex?

A NATIONWIDE survey by *'Teen* magazine revealed that many of its young readers wanted information on the following question: "How to say no to sexual pressure."

At Psalm 119:9, the psalmist posed a similar question: "How will a young man [or woman] cleanse his path?" The answer: "By keeping on guard according to your [God's] word." But more is needed than head knowledge. "You know in your mind what the Bible says about immoral sex," confessed one young woman. "But your heart keeps pushing these reasons into the back of your mind." Appropriately, the psalmist continued: "In my heart I have treasured up your saying, in order that I may not sin against you."—Psalm 119:11.

Safeguard the Heart

To treasure God's sayings in your heart requires first that you read and study the Scriptures and Bible-based literature. This can help convince you of the value of God's laws. On the other hand, reading, listening to, or viewing sexually stimulating material whips up the "sexual appetite." (Colossians 3:5) So strictly avoid such material! Ponder instead on things that are chaste and clean.

Research has further shown that one's close friends can have a great influence on whether one stays chaste. Said the psalmist: "A partner I am of all those who do fear you [God], and of those keeping your orders."—Psalm 119:63.

YOUNG PEOPLE ASK ...

Staying Chaste While Dating

Avoid situations that could lead to necking and petting

Date in groups or have a chaperon

Keep the conversation on an upbuilding level

From the start, let your partner know your attitude regarding limits on expressions of affection

Dress modestly and avoid provocative actions

Ask to be taken home if you feel your chastity is in jeopardy

Refrain from long "good-nights"

Keep an early curfew

Courting couples can pursue activities that do not isolate them from other people

If a situation becomes too "heated," have the sense to say No!—and mean it!

Know your limitations: There are times when you may be more vulnerable to sexual enticements than at other times. For example, you may be discouraged because of some personal failure or a disagreement with your parents. Whatever the case, during such times you will have to be especially cautious. (Proverbs 24:10) Also, be careful about the use of alcoholic beverages. Under the influence of these, you can lose your inhibitions. "Wine and sweet wine are what take away good motive."—Hosea 4:11.

Say no and mean it: What can a couple do when emotions escalate and they find themselves becoming dangerously intimate? One of them has to say or do something that breaks the mood. Debra found herself alone with her date, who stopped the car in a lonely place to "talk." When the emotions began to escalate, Debra said to her date: "Isn't this necking? Shouldn't we stop?" That broke the mood. He immediately drove her home. To say no under these circumstances may be the hardest thing you have ever had to do. But as one 20-year-old woman who gave in to having sexual relations said: "If you don't walk away, you'll be sorry!"

Have a chaperon: Though viewed as old-fashioned by some, having a chaperon to accompany you on a date is still a good idea. "It looks as if we can't be trusted," complain some couples. Perhaps. But is it wise to trust oneself? Proverbs 28:26 bluntly states: "He that is trusting in his own heart is stupid, but he that is walking in wisdom is the one that will escape." Walk wisely by having someone else join you on a date. "I really respect the fellow who brings his own chaperon. I know he is as interested as I am in being chaste," revealed Debra. "It works no hardship, for when we want to say something privately, we just step out of earshot of others. The protection it affords is worth any inconvenience."

Friendship With God

Above all, developing a close friendship with God, knowing him as a real person with feelings, will help you avoid conduct that offends him. Pouring out your heart to him about specific problems draws you close to him. Many couples wishing to remain chaste have even prayed together to God during emotionally charged situations, asking that he give them the needed strength.

Jehovah generously responds by giving such ones "power beyond what is normal." (2 Corinthians 4:7) You, of course, have to do your part. Yet, be assured that with God's help and blessing, it is possible to say no to sexual immorality.

Questions for Discussion   *Chapter 24*

☐ *What are some things you can do that will help you to treasure Jehovah's laws regarding sex?*

☐ *How can your friends affect your view of premarital sex?*

☐ *Why do you feel caution is necessary when dating?*

☐ *What are some things a courting couple can do to protect themselves from falling into sexual immorality?*

Chapter 25

Masturbation —How Serious Is It?

"I'm wondering if masturbation is wrong in the eyes of God. Will it affect my physical and/or mental health in the future and if I ever get married?"—Fifteen-year-old Melissa.

THESE thoughts have plagued many youths. The reason? Masturbation is widespread. Reportedly, some 97 percent of males and more than 90 percent of females have masturbated by the age of 21. Furthermore, this practice has been blamed for all manner of ills—from warts and red eyelids to epilepsy and mental illness.

Though masturbation may cause strong guilt feelings, sincere prayer for God's forgiveness and hard work to resist the practice can give one a good conscience

YOUNG PEOPLE ASK . . .

Twentieth-century medical researchers no longer make such alarming claims. Indeed, doctors today believe that no physical illness is caused by masturbation. Researchers William Masters and Virginia Johnson add that "there is no established medical evidence that masturbation, regardless of frequency, leads to mental illness." Nevertheless, there *are* other ill effects! And many Christian youths are rightly concerned about the practice. "When I gave in to [masturbation], I'd feel as if I were failing Jehovah God," wrote one youth. "I got seriously depressed sometimes."

Just what is masturbation? How serious is it, and why do so many youths find it to be a habit that is hard to break?

Why Youths Are Vulnerable

Masturbation is deliberate self-stimulation to produce sexual arousal. During the bloom of youth, sexual desires become strong. Powerful hormones are released that affect the reproductive organs. A youth thus becomes aware that these organs are capable of producing pleasurable sensations. And sometimes a youth may become sexually excited without even thinking about sex.

For instance, the tensions produced by various worries, fears, or frustrations can affect a boy's sensitive nervous system and cause sexual arousal. A buildup of semen may in turn cause him to awaken sexually excited. Or it may produce a nocturnal emission, usually accompanied by an erotic dream. Similarly, some young girls may find themselves stimulated unintentionally. Many have a heightened sexual desire just before or after their menstrual period.

So if you have experienced such arousal, there is nothing wrong with you. This is a normal response of a youthful body. Such sensations, even if very intense, are not the same as masturbation, since they are largely involuntary. And as you grow older, the intensity of these new sensations will subside.

Curiosity and the novelty of these new sensations, though, lead some youths deliberately to manipulate, or play with, their sexual organs.

'Mental Fuel'

The Bible describes a young man who meets a promiscuous woman. She kisses him and says: "Do come, . . . let us enjoy each other with love expressions." Then what happens? "All of a sudden he is going after her, like a bull that comes even to the slaughter." (Proverbs 7:7-22) Obviously, this youth's passions were aroused not simply because his hormones were at work but because of what he saw and heard.

Some feel the urge to masturbate when under pressure or when tense, lonely, or depressed

Similarly, one young man admits: 'The root of my whole problem with masturbation boiled down to what I put in my mind. I would watch TV programs that included immorality and in some cases watch programs on cable TV that would show nudity. Such scenes are so shocking that they stay with you. They would surface again in my mind, providing the mental fuel needed to engage in masturbation.'

Yes, often it is what one reads, watches, or listens to, as well as what one talks about or meditates on, that triggers masturbation. As one 25-year-old woman confessed: "I just couldn't seem to stop the habit. However, I used to read romance novels, and this contributed to the problem."

A "Tranquilizer"

This young woman's experience reveals what is undoubtedly the greatest reason why the habit can be so hard to break. She continues: "Usually I masturbated to release pressure, tension, or anxiety. That fleeting pleasure was like the drink the alcoholic takes to calm his nerves."

Researchers Suzanne and Irving Sarnoff write: "For some people masturbation may become a habit to which they turn for solace whenever they are rebuffed or feel apprehensive about something. Others, however, may withdraw in this way only occasionally, when they are under the most acute emotional stress." Evidently, others similarly resort to the habit when upset, depressed, lonely, or under much stress; it becomes a "tranquilizer" to blot out their troubles.

What Does the Bible Say?

A youth asked: "Is masturbation an unforgivable sin?" Masturbation is not mentioned at all in the Bible.* The practice was common in the Greek-speaking world during Bible times, and several Greek words were used to describe the practice. But not one of these words is used in the Bible.

Since masturbation is not directly condemned in the Bible, does this mean it is harmless? *Absolutely not!* Though it is not classed with such gross sins as fornication, masturbation is surely an unclean habit. (Ephesians 4:19) The principles of God's Word thus indicate

---

* God executed Onan for 'wasting his semen on the earth.' However, interrupted intercourse, not masturbation, was involved. Furthermore, Onan was executed because he selfishly failed to perform brother-in-law marriage in order to continue his deceased brother's family line. (Genesis 38:1-10) What of the "emission of semen" mentioned at Leviticus 15: 16-18? This apparently refers, not to masturbation, but to a nocturnal emission as well as to marital sexual relations.

that you "benefit yourself" by strongly resisting this unclean habit.—Isaiah 48:17.

Arousing "Sexual Appetite"

"Deaden, therefore, your body members," urges the Bible, "as respects . . . sexual appetite." (Colossians 3:5) "Sexual appetite" refers not to normal sexual feelings but to passion that is out of control. Such "sexual appetite" can thus lead to one's indulging in gross acts, as described by Paul at Romans 1:26, 27.

But does not masturbation "deaden" these desires? No, on the contrary, as one youth confessed: "When you masturbate, you dwell mentally on wrong desires, and all that does is increase your appetite for them." Often an immoral fantasy is used to increase the sexual pleasure. (Matthew 5:27, 28) Therefore, given the right circumstances, one could easily fall into immorality. This happened to one youth, who admits: "At one time, I felt that masturbation could relieve frustration without my getting involved with a female. Yet I developed an overpowering desire to do so." He committed fornication. Not surprisingly, a nationwide study revealed that the majority of adolescents who masturbated were also committing fornication. They outnumbered those who were virgins by 50 percent!

'The root of my whole problem with masturbation boiled down to what I put in my mind'

Mentally and Emotionally Defiling

Masturbation also instills certain attitudes that are mentally corrupting. (Compare 2 Corinthians 11:3.) When masturbating, a person is immersed in his or her own bodily sensations—totally self-centered. Sex becomes separated from love and is relegated to a reflex

Erotic movies, books, and TV shows are often the 'mental fuel' for masturbation

that releases tension. But God intended that sexual desires be satisfied in sexual relations—an expression of love between a man and his wife.—Proverbs 5:15-19.

A masturbator may also tend to view the opposite sex as mere sex objects—tools for sexual satisfaction. Wrong attitudes taught by masturbation thus defile one's "spirit," or dominant mental inclination. In some cases, the problems caused by masturbation persist even after marriage! For good reason, God's Word urges: "Beloved ones, let us cleanse ourselves of every defilement of flesh and spirit."—2 Corinthians 7:1.

A Balanced View of Guilt

Many youths, though generally successful in overcoming this bad habit, occasionally give in to it. Fortunately, God is very merciful. "For you, O Jehovah, are good and ready to forgive," said the psalmist. (Psalm 86:5) When a Christian succumbs to masturbation, his heart is often self-condemning. Yet, the Bible states that "God is greater than our hearts and knows all things." (1 John 3:20) God sees more than our sins. The greatness of his knowledge enables him to hear with sympathy our earnest pleas for forgiveness. As one young woman wrote: "I have felt guilty to an extent, but knowing what a loving God Jehovah is and that he can read my heart and know all my efforts and intentions keeps me from feeling too depressed when I fail on occasion." If you fight the desire to masturbate, it is not likely that you will commit the serious sin of fornication.

The September 1, 1959, issue of *The Watchtower* stated: "We [may] find ourselves stumbling and falling many times over some bad habit that has bitten more deeply into our former pattern of life than we had realized. . . . Do not despair. Do not conclude you have committed the unforgivable sin. That is just how Satan would like you to reason. The fact that you feel grieved and vexed with yourself is proof in itself that you have not gone too far. Never weary of turning humbly and earnestly to God, seeking his forgiveness and cleansing and help. Go to him as a child goes to his father when in trouble, no matter how often on the same weakness, and Jehovah will graciously give you the help because of his undeserved kindness and, if you are sincere, he will give you the realization of a cleansed conscience."

> "*When I gave in to [masturbation], I'd feel as if I were failing Jehovah God*"

How can that "cleansed conscience" be attained?

Questions for Discussion   Chapter 25

☐ What is masturbation, and what are some popular misconceptions regarding it?

☐ Why do youths often feel very strong sexual desire? Do you think this is wrong?

☐ What things can fuel the desire to masturbate?

☐ Does masturbation do a youth any harm?

☐ How serious a sin do you feel masturbation is? How does Jehovah view a youth who is putting up a fight against it, though perhaps having problems overcoming it?

Chapter 26

Masturbation—How Can I Fight the Urge?

"IT IS a very strong addiction," said a young man who struggled with masturbation for over 15 years. "It can be just as habit forming as any drug or alcoholic beverage."

The apostle Paul, however, did not let his desires become like a harsh master. On the contrary, he wrote: "I pummel my body [fleshly desires] and lead it as a slave." (1 Corinthians 9:27) He got tough with himself! A similar effort will enable *anyone* to break free from masturbation.

"Prepare Your Minds for Action"

Many masturbate to relieve tension and anxiety. Masturbation, though, is a childish way to react to problems. (Compare 1 Corinthians 13:11.) Better it is to show "thinking ability" and attack the problem itself. (Proverbs 1:4) When problems and frustrations seem overwhelming, "throw all your anxiety upon [God]." —1 Peter 5:6, 7.

Suppose you accidentally see or hear something that is sexually stimulating? The Bible recommends: "Prepare your minds for action; be self-controlled." (1 Peter 1:13, *New International Version*) Exert your mind and *reject* the immoral thought. The arousal will soon die down.

Rejecting bad thoughts is especially difficult, though, when one is alone at night. One young woman advises:

"Prayer is an instant tower of strength. Praying at the time the desire arises definitely helps"

"The best thing to do is get right out of bed and get busy with some type of work, or maybe have a little snack, so that *your mind turns to other things.*" Yes, force yourself to 'consider whatever things are of serious concern, righteous, chaste, lovable, well spoken of.'—Philippians 4:8.

When you have difficulty falling asleep, endeavor to imitate faithful King David, who wrote: "When I have remembered you [God] upon my lounge, during the night watches I meditate on you." (Psalm 63:6) Forcing your mind to ponder on God and his qualities will often break the spell. It also helps if you keep thinking of how God views this unclean habit.—Psalm 97:10.

Take Preventive Measures

"Shrewd is the one that has seen the calamity and proceeds to conceal himself, but the inexperienced have passed along and must suffer the penalty," wrote the inspired wise man. (Proverbs 22:3) You can show yourself shrewd by exercising forethought. For example, if you find that engaging in certain activities, wearing tight-fitting clothing, or eating certain foods has caused you to become sexually stimulated, then by all means avoid such. Alcoholic drinks, for example, can lower one's inhibitions and make self-control harder. Also, avoid like the plague any reading matter, TV programs, or movies with sensuous themes. "Make my

YOUNG PEOPLE ASK . . .

eyes pass on from seeing what is worthless," prayed the psalmist.—Psalm 119:37.

Preventive measures can also be taken for those times when you are particularly vulnerable. A young woman may find that her sexual desires become more intense at certain times of the month. Or one may be emotionally hurt or depressed. "Have you shown yourself discouraged in the day of distress? Your power will be scanty," warns Proverbs 24:10. So avoid being alone for long periods of time. Plan upbuilding activities that will keep your mind involved in challenging undertakings, giving it less opportunity to gravitate toward immoral thoughts.

A Spiritual Offensive

A 27-year-old man who had struggled with the habit since he was 11 was finally able to gain the victory. "It was a matter of going on the offensive," he explained. "I read the Bible, at least two chapters *every single day* without exception." He has done this without fail for over three years. Advises yet another Christian: "Before going to bed, read something related to spiritual things. It is very important that the last thought of the day be a spiritual one. Prayer at this time is also *extremely* helpful."

"Having plenty to do in the work of the Lord," such as the work of teaching others the Bible, also helps. (1 Corinthians 15:58) One woman who overcame masturbation stated: "One thing that now really helps me to avoid this habit is that as a full-time evangelizer my mind and energies are all turned toward helping others to gain an approved relationship with God."

By heartfelt prayer, you can also beg God for "the power beyond what is normal." (2 Corinthians 4:7) "Before him [God] pour out your heart." (Psalm 62:8)

*P*ornography—Habit-Forming and Dangerous!

*"**Pornography** is everywhere: you walk down the street—there it is displayed openly on newsstands,"* recalled 19-year-old Ronald. "Some of our teachers would bring it to school, reading it at their desks while waiting for the next class." Yes, many people of various ages, backgrounds, and educational levels are avid readers of pornography. A youth named Mark said: "When I read girlie magazines and viewed the photographs it was exciting! . . . I looked forward to new issues of these magazines because going through ones I had finished didn't give me the same flush of excitement. It's habit-forming." But is it a good habit?

Pornography has an overwhelming message: 'Sex is purely for self-gratification.' Much of it is saturated with rape and sadistic violence. Many viewers soon find that "milder" forms (soft-core) are

no longer stimulating and so they seek out pictures or movies that are even more obscene! As Ernest van den Haag, an assistant professor at New York University, said: "Pornography invites us to perceive others only as pieces of meat, as objects of exploitation for the sake of our own sensations of pleasure."

Pornography further presents a warped, idolized view of sex that often leads to marital problems. Says one young wife: "Reading pornography caused me to desire with my husband the abnormal things portrayed in the books. This led to constant frustration and a letdown sexually." A 1981 survey was conducted among several hundred women regarding the effects of pornography on their rapport with the men in their lives who read it. Nearly one half reported that it caused serious problems. It actually destroyed some marriages or engagements. One wife lamented: "I can only assume by [my husband's] need and desire for sexual release with pornography that I am inadequate . . . I wish to God I were a woman who could satisfy him, but he prefers plastic and paper and his need has destroyed a part of me. . . . Pornography is . . . anti-love . . . It is ugly, cruel and destructive."

Of greatest concern to Christian youths, however, is the fact that pornography directly works against one's efforts to be clean in God's sight. (2 Corinthians 6:17– 7:1) The Bible shows that "because of the insensibility of their hearts" some in ancient times came "to be past all moral sense" and "gave themselves over to loose conduct to work uncleanness of every sort with greediness." (Ephesians 4:18, 19) Would you want to experience such corruption? Remember, even an occasional indulgence in pornography can have a desensitizing effect on one's conscience. It has led some young Christians to mastur-

bation and, worse yet, sexual immorality. The wise thing, then, is to work hard to stay free from pornography.

"Many times pornography is in my direct line of sight," says young Darryl. "So I am forced to see it at first glance; but I don't have to look a second time." Yes, refuse to look where it is openly displayed, and refuse to allow classmates to goad you into looking at it. As 18-year-old Karen reasoned: "As an imperfect person it is difficult enough trying to keep my mind on things that are chaste and praiseworthy. Would it not be all the more difficult if I deliberately read pornography?"

One young woman says: "Prayer is an instant tower of strength. Praying at the time the desire arises definitely helps." Also, upon rising and throughout the day, express your resolve to God and plead for his strengthening holy spirit.—Luke 11:13.

Help From Others

If your personal efforts are not successful, speak to someone who can help, such as a parent or a Christian elder. Young women may find it helpful to confide in a mature Christian woman. (Titus 2:3-5) One young man who was at the point of despair said: "I talked privately with my father one evening about it." He revealed: "It took everything I had to tell him. I cried as I told him, I was so ashamed. But I'll never forget what he said. With a reassuring smile on his face, he said: 'You make me so proud of you.' He knew what I had to go through to get to that point. No words could have lifted my spirits and determination more.

"My father then showed me a few scriptures to help me see that I was not 'too far gone,'" continued the youth, "and then some more scriptures to be sure I understood the seriousness of my wrong course. He said to 'keep the slate clean' until a certain time, and we would discuss it again then. He told me not to let it crush me if I relapsed, just go a longer period of time without giving in the next time." After overcoming the problem fully, the young man added: "Having someone else aware of my problem and helping me was the greatest benefit."

Dealing With a Relapse

After working hard to overcome the habit, one youth suffered a relapse. He admitted: "It was like a crushing weight on me. I felt so unworthy. I then rationalized: 'I'm too far gone. I don't have Jehovah's favor anyhow, so why be tough on myself?'" However, a relapse does not mean that one has lost the fight. One 19-year-old girl recalls: "At first it happened about every night, but then I began relying on Jehovah more, and with the help of his spirit I now only fail maybe six times a year. I feel very bad afterward, but each time I fail, when the next temptation comes, I'm much stronger." So *gradually* she is winning her fight.

When a relapse occurs, analyze what led up to it. One youth says: "I review what I have been reading or thinking about. Almost always I can pinpoint the reason I slipped. This way I can stop doing that and correct it."

The Rewards of a Good Fight

Said one youth who overcame masturbation: "Since overcoming the problem, I can keep a clean conscience before Jehovah, and that is something that I wouldn't trade for anything!"

Yes, a good conscience, an improved sense of self-worth, greater moral strength, and a closer relationship with God are all rewards of a good fight against masturbation. Says one young woman who finally overcame masturbation: "Believe me, the victory over this habit is well worth the effort put forth."

Questions for Discussion   Chapter 26

☐ *Why is it dangerous to dwell on erotic thoughts? What can a youth do to get his or her mind onto something else?*

☐ *What preventive measures might a youth take to lessen the temptation to indulge in masturbation?*

☐ *Why is a spiritual offensive helpful?*

☐ *What role does prayer play in overcoming this habit?*

☐ *Why is it helpful to confide in someone if there is a problem in this regard?*

Chapter 27

Honesty—Is It Really the Best Policy?

HAVE you ever been tempted to lie? Donald told his mother that he had cleaned his room when, in reality, he had thrown everything under the bed. Richard made an equally inept attempt at pulling the wool over his parents' eyes. He told them that he got a failing grade, not because he did not study, but because he 'did not get along with his teacher.'

Parents and other adults usually see through such transparent ploys. Yet that does not stop many youths from at least *trying* to lie, bend the truth, or downright cheat when it seems advantageous. For one thing, parents do not always react coolly to crises. And when you have come in two hours later than you were supposed to, it may seem tempting to say there was a major accident on the freeway, rather than to tell your parents the embarrassing truth —that you simply lost track of the time.

> '*A*ny student committing an act of academic dishonesty will run a serious risk of harming future opportunities'

School may present another challenge to honesty. Students often feel overloaded with homework. Cutthroat competition often exists. Why, in the United States, surveys show that more than half of all students cheat or have cheated. But while a lie may seem attractive, and cheating the easy way out, does it really pay to be dishonest?

212   *YOUNG PEOPLE ASK . . .*

Lying—Why It Doesn't Pay

Lying to escape punishment might seem advantageous at the time. But the Bible warns: "He that launches forth lies will not escape." (Proverbs 19:5) The likelihood is great that the lie will be exposed and punishment meted out anyway. Then your parents will be angry not only because of your original transgression but also because of your lying to them!

What about cheating in school? Says a director of campus judicial programs: "Any student committing an act of academic dishonesty will run a serious risk of harming future educational and employment opportunities."

True, many seem to be getting away with it. Cheating may very well get you that passing grade, but what are the long-range effects? You no doubt agree it would

Parents will usually see through lame attempts to explain away disobedience

be foolish to cheat your way through a class on swimming. After all, who wants to be stuck on land when everybody else is having fun in the water! And if you got pushed into a pool, your cheating habits could cause you to drown!

But what about cheating at math or reading? True, the results may not be quite as dramatic—at first. If you have not developed basic academic skills, however, you may find yourself "sinking" in the job market! And a diploma obtained by cheating won't be much of a life preserver. The Bible says: "The getting of treasures by a false tongue is an exhalation driven away." (Proverbs 21:6) Any advantages a lie may bring are as short-lived as vapor. How much better it would be for you to buckle down and study, rather than to lie and cheat your way through school! "The plans of the diligent one surely make for advantage," says Proverbs 21:5.

Lying and Your Conscience

A young girl named Michelle lyingly accused her brother of breaking a cherished knickknack, though she later felt compelled to confess her lie to her parents. "I felt really bad most of the time," explains Michelle. "My parents had put trust in me, and I let them down." This well illustrates how God has placed within mankind the faculty of conscience. (Romans 2:14, 15) Michelle's conscience tormented her with guilt feelings.

Of course, a person could choose to ignore his conscience. But the more he practices lying, the more he becomes insensitive to the wrong—'marked in his conscience as with a branding iron.' (1 Timothy 4:2) Do you really want to have a deadened conscience?

God's View of Lying

"A false tongue" was and is one of the things that "Jehovah does hate." (Proverbs 6:16, 17) After all, it is Satan the Devil himself who is "the father of the lie." (John 8:44) And the Bible makes no distinction between lies and so-called white lies. "No lie originates with the truth."—1 John 2:21.

Honesty must thus be the policy for anyone who wants to be God's friend. The 15th Psalm asks: "O Jehovah, who will be a guest in your tent? Who will reside in your holy mountain?" (Verse 1) Let us consider the answer given in the next four verses:

"He who is walking faultlessly and practicing righteousness and speaking the truth in his heart." (Verse 2) Does that sound like a shoplifter or a cheater? Is it someone who lies to his parents or pretends to be something he is not? Hardly! So if you want to be a friend of God, you need to be honest, not only in your actions but in your *heart* as well.

"He has not slandered with his tongue. To his companion he has done nothing bad, and no reproach has he taken up against his intimate acquaintance." (Verse 3) Have you ever allowed yourself to go along with a group

of youths who were making unkind, cutting comments about someone else? Develop the strength of willpower to refuse to participate in such talk!

"In his eyes anyone contemptible is certainly rejected, but those fearing Jehovah he honors. He has sworn to what is bad for himself, and yet he does not alter." (Verse 4) Reject as friends any youths who lie, cheat, or

The Bible makes no distinction between lies and so-called white lies

brag about immoral exploits; they will expect you to do the same things. As a youth named Bobby observed: "A friend you lie along with will get you in trouble. He is not a friend you can trust." Find friends who respect standards of honesty.—Compare Psalm 26:4.

Did you notice that Jehovah appreciates, or "honors," those who keep their word? Perhaps you promised to help out around the house this Saturday, but now you have been invited to a ball game for that afternoon. Will you treat your word lightly and go with your friends, leaving your parents to do the chores, or will you keep your word?

"His money he has not given out on interest, and a bribe against the innocent one he has not taken. He that is doing these things will never be made to totter." (Verse 5) Isn't it true that greed is a major cause of cheating and dishonesty? Students who cheat on tests are greedy for grades they have not studied for. People who take bribes value money more than justice.

True, some point to political and business leaders who bend rules of honesty to get their way. But how solid is the success of such persons? Answers Psalm 37:2: "Like grass they will speedily wither, and like green new grass they will fade away." If not caught and disgraced by others, ultimately they face the judgment of Jehovah God. God's friends, however, "will *never* be made to totter." Their eternal future is assured.

Developing "an Honest Conscience"

Is there not strong reason, then, to avoid *any* kind of lying? The apostle Paul said of himself and his companions: "We trust we have an honest conscience." (Hebrews 13:18) Is your conscience likewise sensitive to untruth? If not, train it by studying the Bible and Bible-based literature such as *The Watchtower* and *Awake!*

Young Bobby has done so, with good results. He has learned not to cover over problems with a web of lies. His conscience prods him to approach his parents and honestly discuss matters. At times this has resulted in his receiving discipline. Nevertheless, he admits that he 'feels better inside' for having been honest.

Speaking the truth is not always easy. But the one who makes a decision to tell the truth will maintain a good conscience, a good relationship with his real friends, and best of all, the privilege of being a "guest" in the tent of God! Honesty, then, is not only the best policy, it is the *right* policy for all Christians.

Questions for Discussion	*Chapter 27*

□ *What are some situations in which it might seem tempting to lie?*

□ *Why doesn't it pay to lie or cheat? Can you illustrate this from personal observation or experience?*

□ *How does a liar damage his conscience?*

□ *Read Psalm 15. How do the verses apply to the issue of honesty?*

□ *How can a youth develop an honest conscience?*

Dating, Love, and the Opposite Sex

You've begun to notice the opposite sex—perhaps even one person in particular. New feelings and emotions surge through your body. But just what is it that you are feeling? Is it love —the kind that lasts forever—or something else? And just what should you do about those feelings? Let us now examine some sensible answers to your questions on the subject of romance.

Chapter 28

How Can I Get Over a Crush?

"FOR most teens," wrote one youth-oriented magazine, "crushes are as common as colds." Almost all youths experience them, and almost all manage to survive to adulthood, with their pride and sense of humor intact. However, when you are caught in the grip of a crush, there is little to laugh about. "I was frustrated," recalls one youth, "because I couldn't *do* anything about it. I knew she was too old for me, but I liked her. I was really bent out of shape over the whole thing."

The Anatomy of a Crush

It is no sin to have strong feelings for someone —provided such are not immoral or improper (such as for someone married). (Proverbs 5:15-18) When you are young, though, "desires incidental to youth" often rule your thoughts and actions. (2 Timothy 2:22) Still learning to control the new and potent desires unleashed by puberty, a youth can be full of whipped-up romantic feelings—and have no one to lavish them on.

Furthermore, "girls become poised and socially at ease at an earlier age than boys." As a result, "they often find their male classmates immature and unexciting compared to teachers" or other older, unattainable men. (*Seventeen* magazine) A girl might thus imagine that a favorite teacher, pop singer, or some older acquaintance is the "ideal" man. Boys often become similarly infatuated. However, the love felt for such distant figures is obviously rooted more in fantasy than reality.

Crushes—Why They Can Be Harmful

While most crushes are amazingly short-lived, still they can do a lot of damage to a youth. For one thing, many objects of teenage affection are simply not worthy of esteem. A wise man said: "Foolishness has been put in many high positions." (Ecclesiastes 10:6) Thus a singer is idolized because he has a smooth voice or striking looks. But are his morals worth praising? Is he or she "in the Lord" as a dedicated Christian?—1 Corinthians 7:39.

The Bible also warns: "Friendship with the world is enmity with God." (James 4:4) Would it not jeopardize your friendship with God if you set your heart on a person whose conduct God condemns? Too, the Bible commands, "Guard yourselves from idols." (1 John 5:21) What would you call it when a youth decorates his or her room wall to wall with pictures of a singing star? Would not the word "idolatry" fit? How could this possibly please God?

Some youths even allow their fantasies to override reason. One young woman says: "Whenever I ask him how he feels—he always denies having any feelings for me. But I can tell by the way he looks and acts that this isn't true." The young man in question has tried to be

Crushes on older, unavailable members of the opposite sex are quite common

kind in expressing his disinterest, but she just won't take no for an answer.

Writes another girl of her infatuation with a popular singer: 'I want him to be my boyfriend, and I have prayed that it come true! I used to sleep with his album because that was the closest I could get to him. I'm at the point where if I can't have him, I'll *kill myself.*' Could such mindless passion be pleasing to God, who commands us to serve him with "a sound mind"?—Romans 12:3.

Says the Bible at Proverbs 13:12: "Expectation postponed is making the heart sick." Cultivating romantic expectations for an impossible relationship is thus unhealthy, unrequited love being cited by doctors as a cause of "depression, anxiety, and general distress . . . sleeplessness or lethargy, chest pains or breathlessness." (Compare 2 Samuel 13:1, 2.) One infatuated girl confesses: "I can't eat. . . . I can't study anymore. I . . . daydream about him. . . . I'm miserable."

Think of the havoc you wreak when you allow a fantasy to dominate your life. Dr. Lawrence Bauman observes that one of the first evidences of a runaway crush is a "slackening off of school effort." Isolation from friends and family is another common result. There can also be humiliation. "I'm embarrassed to

Taking a cool, objective look at this person may cure you of your romantic notions

admit this," says writer Gil Schwartz, "but I behaved like a buffoon during my crush on Judy." Long after the crush has dissipated, memories of your following someone around, making a scene in public, and in general making a fool of yourself can linger.

Facing Reality

King Solomon, one of the wisest men who ever lived, fell desperately in love with a girl who did not return his feelings. He poured upon her some of the most beautiful poetry ever written, telling her she was "beautiful like the full moon, pure like the glowing sun" —and got absolutely nowhere with her!—Song of Solomon 6:10.

Nevertheless, Solomon eventually quit his attempts to win her over. How can you, too, regain control of your feelings? "He that is trusting in his own heart is stupid," says the Bible. (Proverbs 28:26) This is particularly true when you are caught up in a romantic fantasy. However, "he that is walking in wisdom is the one that will escape." This means seeing things the way they are.

"How do you tell legitimate hope from unfounded hope?" asks Dr. Howard Halpern. "By looking carefully and coldly at the facts." Consider: How much of a chance is there of a real romance developing with this person? If the person is a celebrity, the odds are you will never even meet this person! Your chances are equally dim when some older person, such as a teacher, is involved.

Furthermore, has the person you like thus far shown any interest in you at all? If not, is there any *real reason* to believe that things will change in the future? Or are you simply reading romantic interest into innocent words and actions on his or her part? Incidentally, in most lands it is customary for men to take the initiative in romance.

A young girl can humiliate herself by aggressively pursuing someone who simply is not interested.

Besides, what would you do if the person actually returned your affections? Are you ready for the responsibilities of marriage? If not, then "remove vexation from your heart" by refusing to dwell on fantasy. There is "a time to love," and that might be years later when you are older.—Ecclesiastes 3:8; 11:10.

Analyzing Your Feelings

Dr. Charles Zastrow observes: "Infatuation occurs when a person idealizes the person she or he is infatuated with as being a 'perfect lover'; that is, concludes that the other person has *all* of the characteristics desired in a mate." However, no such "perfect lover" exists. "For all have sinned and fall short of the glory of God," says the Bible.—Romans 3:23.

can't eat. can't study anymore. daydream ut him. I'm serable'

So ask yourself: How well do I really know this person I have set heart on? Am I in love with an image? Am I blinding myself to this person's flaws? One objective look at your dream lover may be enough to pull you out of your romantic stupor! It is also helpful to analyze the kind of love you feel for this person. Says writer Kathy McCoy: "*Immature love* can come and go in a moment . . . The focus is on you, and you're simply in love with the idea of being in love . . . *Immature love* is clinging, possessive, and jealous. . . . *Immature love* demands perfection."—Contrast 1 Corinthians 13:4, 5.

Getting Him or Her Off Your Mind

Admittedly, all the reasoning in the world does not entirely erase how you feel. But you can avoid feeding the problem. Reading steamy romance novels, watching TV love stories, or just listening to certain kinds of music can worsen your feelings of loneliness. So refuse to dwell on the situation. "Where there is no wood the fire goes out."—Proverbs 26:20.

A fantasy romance is no substitute for people who really love you and care for you. Do not 'isolate yourself.' (Proverbs 18:1) You'll probably find that your parents can be quite helpful. For all your attempts to conceal your feelings, they have probably already discerned that something is eating away at you. Why not approach them and give your heart to them? (Comp Proverbs 23:26.) A mature Christian may also pro have a good listening ear.

"Keep busy," exhorts teen writer Esther Davido Take up a hobby, do some exercise, study a langu begin a Bible research project. Staying engrosse useful activities can ease the withdrawal sympt quite a bit.

Getting over a crush is not easy. But with the pass of time, the pain will subside. You will have learned m about yourself and your feelings, and you will be be prepared to deal with *real love* should it come in future! But how will you be able to recognize 'real love

---

Questions for Discussion   Chapter

☐ *Why are crushes common among youths?*

☐ *Who often are the objects of youthful romantic fantasies, an why?*

☐ *Why can crushes be harmful?*

☐ *What are some things a youth can do to get over a crush?*

☐ *How can a youth avoid feeding a romantic fantasy?*

*Y*ouths often feel
pressured to date
or pair off

with a member of the opposite sex, the more sexual desire can grow—whether you want it to or not. (See pages 232-3.) It is the way all of us are made! Until you are older and more in control of your feelings, dating may simply be too much for you to handle. Unfortunately, many youths find this out the hard way.

"When we started dating, . . . we didn't even hold hands or kiss. I just wanted to enjoy the pleasure of her company and talk," said one young man. "However, she was very affectionate and would sit very close to me. In time we did hold hands and kiss. This created within me an even stronger sex drive. It affected my thinking to the point that I wanted to be with her, not just to talk, but to hold her, touch her and kiss. I couldn't get enough! I was literally going crazy with passion. At times I would feel cheap and ashamed."

Little wonder, then, that dating often culminates in

Dating often puts youths under pressure to grant unwanted displays of affection

One can enjoy the company of the opposite sex in circumstances free of the pressures of dating

illicit sexual relations. A survey of several hundred teenagers found that 87 percent of the girls and 95 percent of the boys felt that sex was either "moderately important or very important" in dating. However, 65 percent of the girls and 43 percent of the boys admitted that there had been times on a date when they had had sexual contact even though they did not feel like it!

Recalls 20-year-old Loretta: "The more we saw each other, the more involved we became. Kissing soon grew stale and we began touching intimate body parts. I became a nervous wreck because I felt so dirty. My date also in time expected me to 'go all the way' . . . I was confused and bewildered. But all I could think of was, 'I don't want to lose him.' I was miserable!"

True, not every couple end up having sexual relations; some let their displays of affection stop just short of it. But what results when one is worked up emotionally and has no honorable outlet for such feelings? Guaranteed frustration. And those frustrations are not limited to sexual feelings.

Torn Emotions

Consider one young man's dilemma: 'I liked Kathy a lot at first. Well, I admit I talked her into doing some things she didn't think were right. Now I feel dirty because I've lost interest. How can I ditch Kathy without hurting her feelings?' What a perplexing situation! And how would you feel if you were Kathy?

Teen heartbreak is a common malady. True, a young couple walking hand in hand may present an attractive picture. But what are the odds that the same

So-called platonic relationships often end in heartbreak

couple will still be together a year from now, much less married to each other? Slim indeed. Teen romances are thus almost always doomed relationships, seldom culminating in marriage, often terminating in heartbreak.

After all, during the teen years your personality is still in a state of flux. You are discovering who you are, what you really like, what you want to do with your life. Someone who interests you today may very well bore you tomorrow. But when romantic feelings have been allowed to flourish, someone is bound to get hurt. Not surprisingly, several research studies have linked "a fight with a girl friend" or "disappointment in love" as among the situations responsible for many youthful suicides.

> *"Kissing soon grew stale and we began touching intimate body parts. I became a nervous wreck because I felt so dirty. My date also in time expected me to 'go all the way'"*

Am I Ready?

God tells young people: "Rejoice, young man [or woman], in your youth, and let your heart do you good in the days of your young manhood, and walk in the ways of your heart and in the things seen by your eyes." Young people do tend to "walk in the ways of [their] heart." Yet so often those "ways," which seem to be such fun, end up bringing vexation and calamity. The Bible thus urges in the following verse: "Remove vexation from your heart, and ward off calamity from your flesh; for youth and the prime of life are vanity." (Ecclesiastes 11:9, 10) "Vexation" refers to being deeply troubled or sorely distressed. "Calamity" denotes a personal disaster. Both can make life miserable.

Does this mean, then, that dating itself is a source of

*C*an a Boy and a Girl 'Just Be Friends'?

So-called platonic relationships (affectionate relationships between men and women into which the sexual element does not enter) are quite popular among youths. Claims 17-year-old Gregory: "It's easier for me to talk to girls because they're usually more sympathetic and sensitive." Other youngsters argue that such friendships help them develop a more rounded-out personality.

The Bible urges young men to treat "younger women as sisters with all chasteness." (1 Timothy 5:2) By applying this principle, it is indeed possible to enjoy clean, wholesome friendships with members of the opposite sex. The apostle Paul, for example, was a single man who enjoyed a number of friendships with Christian women. (See Romans 16:1, 3, 6, 12.) He wrote of two "women who have striven side by side with me in the good news." (Philippians 4:3) Jesus Christ also enjoyed balanced, wholesome association with women. On numerous occasions, he en-

joyed the hospitality and conversation of Martha and Mary. —Luke 10:38, 39; John 11:5.

Nevertheless, a "platonic" friendship is often little more than a thinly disguised romance or a way to get attention from someone of the opposite sex without commitment. And since feelings can easily change, there is a need for caution. Warned Dr. Marion Hilliard: "An easy companionship traveling at about ten miles an hour can shift without warning to a blinding passion going a hundred miles an hour."

Sixteen-year-old Mike learned this when he became "friends" with a 14-year-old girl: "I quickly found out [that] two people cannot stay just friends when they keep seeing each other exclusively. Our relationship kept growing and growing. We soon had special feelings for each other, and we still do." Since neither is old enough to marry, those feelings are a source of frustration.

Too much close association can have yet sadder conse-

you really know how your friend feels about you?

In his book The Friendship Factor, *Alan Loy McGinnis advises: "Don't trust yourself too far." Take precautions, perhaps confining your association to properly supervised group activities. Avoid inappropriate displays of affection or being alone in romantic circumstances. When you are troubled, confide in parents and older persons rather than a youth of the opposite sex.*

quences. One youth tried to comfort a female friend who confided in him about some of her problems. Before long, they were petting. The result? Troubled consciences and bad feelings between them. With others, sexual relations have resulted. A survey taken by Psychology Today revealed: "Almost half the respondents (49 percent) have had a friendship turn into a sexual relationship." In fact, "nearly a third (31 percent) reported having had sexual intercourse with a friend in the past month."

'**But** *I'm not attracted to my friend and would never get romantically involved with him [or her].' Perhaps. But how might you feel in the future? Besides, "he that is trusting in his own heart is stupid." (Proverbs 28:26) Our hearts can be treacherous, deceptive, blinding us to our true motives. And do*

And what if, in spite of safeguards, unshared romantic feelings develop? "Speak truth," and let the other person know where you stand. (Ephesians 4:25) If this does not settle matters, it might be best to keep your distance. "Shrewd is the one that has seen the calamity and proceeds to conceal himself." (Proverbs 22:3) Or as the book The Friendship Factor *puts it: "Bail out if necessary. Once in a while, no matter how much we try, a friendship with the opposite sex gets out of hand and we know where it is going to lead." Then, it is time to "back away."*

vexation and calamity? Not necessarily. But it can be if you date for a wrong reason ('for fun') or before you are ready for it! The following questions may, therefore, prove helpful in evaluating your own situation.

Would dating help or hinder my emotional growth? Dating can limit you to a boy-girl relationship. Might it not benefit you, instead, to widen out in your association with others? (Compare 2 Corinthians 6:12, 13.) A young woman named Susan says: "I learned to develop close friendships with older Christian women in the congregation. They needed companionship, and I needed their steadying influence. So I would drop in for coffee. We would talk and laugh. I made real, lifelong friendships with them."

'How can I ditch Kathy without hurting her feelings?'

By having many types of friends—old and young, single and married, male and female—you learn to be poised around people, including those of the opposite sex, with much less pressure than on a date. Furthermore, by associating with married couples, you gain a more realistic view of marriage. Later on you will be better prepared to select a good mate and fulfill your own role in marriage. (Proverbs 31:10) A youth named Gail thus concludes: "I'm not ready to get married and settle down. I'm still getting to know myself, and I have many spiritual goals yet to achieve. So I really don't need to be too close to anyone of the opposite sex."

Do I want to cause hurt feelings? Both your feelings and those of the other person can be crushed if romantic bonds are forged with no prospect of marriage in sight. Really, is it fair to heap romantic attention upon someone in order to gain experience with the opposite sex?—See Matthew 7:12.

234   *YOUNG PEOPLE ASK . . .*

What do my parents say? Parents often see dangers to which you are blind. After all, they were young once. They know what real problems can develop when two young people of the opposite sex start spending a lot of time together! So if your parents disapprove of your dating, do not rebel. (Ephesians 6:1-3) Likely, they simply feel you should wait till you are older.

Will I be able to follow the Bible's morality? When one is "past the bloom of youth," one can better deal with sexual impulses—and even then it is not easy. Are you really ready at this point in life to handle a close relationship with someone of the opposite sex and keep it chaste?

Interestingly, many youths are asking themselves these questions and coming to the same conclusion reached by Mary Ann (quoted earlier). She said: "I determined that I was not going to be influenced about dating by the attitudes of others. I was not going to date till I was old enough and ready to get married and I saw someone with the qualities I wanted in a husband."

Mary Ann thus raises *the* critical question you must ask yourself before dating.

Questions for Discussion   *Chapter 29*

□ *What does the term "dating" mean to you?*

□ *Why do some youths feel under pressure to date?*

□ *Why is dating unwise for someone in "the bloom of youth"?*

□ *How can a youth "ward off calamity" when it comes to dating?*

□ *What are some problems that can develop when a boy and a girl are 'just friends'?*

□ *How can you know if you're ready to date?*

Chapter 30

Am I Ready for Marriage?

MARRIAGE is not a game. God intended for husbands and wives to forge a permanent bond, closer than that with any other human. (Genesis 2:24) A marriage mate is thus someone you will stick to—or be stuck with—for the rest of your life.

Any marriage is sure to suffer some "pain and grief." (1 Corinthians 7:28, *The New English Bible*) But Marcia Lasswell, who is a professor of behavioral science, warns: "If there is one unchallenged bit of information we have concerning whether or not a marriage will last, it is that those who are very young when they marry have three strikes against them."

Why do so many young marriages fail? The answer to this may have a strong bearing on determining whether *you* are ready for marriage or not.

Great Expectations

"We had a very poor idea of what marriage was," admits one teenage girl. "We thought we could come and go, do as we pleased, do or not do the dishes, but it isn't that way." Many youths nurture such immature views of marriage. They imagine it to be a romantic fantasy. Or they head for the altar because they want the status of appearing grown up. Yet others simply want to escape a bad situation at home, at school, or in their community. Confided one girl to her fiancé: "I'll be so glad when we get married. Then I won't ever have to make any more decisions!"

But marriage is neither a fantasy nor a cure-all for problems. If anything, it presents a whole new set of problems to deal with. "Many teenagers get married to play house," says Vicky, who had her first child at 20. "Oh, it looks like such fun! You think of a child as a little doll, something that is so cute and that you can just play with, but that's not the way it is."

Many youths also have unrealistic expectations regarding sexual relations. Said one young man who married at age 18: "After I got married I found out that the great thrill of sex wears off very soon and then we started having some real problems." One study of teenage couples found that second to financial problems, most arguments were over sexual relations. Doubtless this is because satisfying marital relations result from unselfishness and self-control—qualities youths have often failed to cultivate.—1 Corinthians 7:3, 4.

Wisely, the Bible encourages Christians to marry when they are "past the bloom of youth." (1 Corinthians 7:36) Marrying when passion is at high tide can distort

Many youths enter marriage little more prepared for it than these

237

your thinking and blind you to a prospective mate's flaws.

Unready for Their Roles

One teenage bride says of her husband: "Now that we are married, the only time he acts interested in me is when he wants sex. He thinks his boyfriends are just as important to be with as I am. . . . I thought I was going to be his one and only, but was I fooled." This highlights a misconception that is common among young men: They think that as husbands, they can still live the life-style of single men.

A 19-year-old bride points to a problem common among young wives: "I'd rather watch TV and sleep than clean house and fix meals. I'm ashamed when my husband's parents visit because they keep a nice house and mine is always a mess. I'm a lousy cook, too." What stress it can add to a marriage when a girl is incompetent domestically! "Marriage really takes commitment," stated Vicky (previously quoted). "This isn't a game. The fun of the wedding is over. It soon becomes day-to-day living and that isn't easy."

And what about the day-to-day grind of supporting a family? Vicky's husband, Mark, says: "I remember that for my first job I had to get up at 6 a.m. I kept thinking:

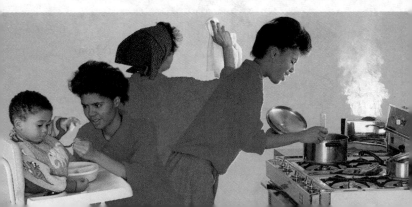

'This is hard work. Will I ever get some relief?' And then when I got home I felt that Vicky didn't understand what I was going through."

Money Problems

This brings us to another cause of marital discord for young married couples: money. Forty-eight teenage couples admitted that after three months of marriage, their biggest problem was "spending family income." After nearly three years, 37 of these couples were asked the same question. Money problems were number one again—and their anguish was even worse! "What fun can you get out of life," asked Bill, "when you never have enough money to buy the things you need to make you content? . . . When you don't have enough to last from one payday to another, it can start lots of fights and unhappiness."

Money problems are common among teenagers, as they often have the highest rate of unemployment and the lowest wages. "Because I couldn't provide for my family, we had to live with my parents," admitted Roy. "This created real tension, especially since we had a child as well." Proverbs 24:27 advises: "Prepare your work out of doors, and make it ready for yourself in the field. Afterward you must also build up your household." In Bible times, men worked hard to be in a position later to support a family. Having failed to make such adequate preparations, many young husbands today find the role of provider a burdensome one.

But even a good-size paycheck will not end money problems if a couple have a childish view of material things. One study revealed that "teenagers expected to be able to purchase immediately for their projected family units many of the items that probably had taken their parents years to acquire." Determined to enjoy these material things now, many plunged deeply into debt. Lacking the maturity to be content with "sustenance and covering," they increased stress in their marriage.—1 Timothy 6:8-10.

"Miles Apart"

Maureen recalls: "I was in love with Don. He was so handsome, so strong, such a good athlete and very popular . . . Our marriage *had* to work." But it did not. Resentment built up to the point where, as Maureen says, "Everything Don did irritated me—even the way he smacked his lips when we ate. Finally, we both couldn't take it anymore." Their marriage collapsed within two years.

> *"If there is one unchallenged bit of information we have concerning whether or not a marriage will last, it is that those who are very young when they marry have three strikes against them."—Marcia Lasswell, a professor of behavioral science*

The problem? "Our life goals were miles apart," explained Maureen. "I now realized that I needed someone I could relate to intellectually. But Don's whole life was sports. The things that I thought were so important at 18 suddenly meant nothing to me."

Youths often have a childish view of what they want in a marriage mate, making good looks a priority. Proverbs 31:30 warns: "Charm may be false, and prettiness may be vain."

Making a Self-Examination

The Bible calls rash the person who makes a solemn vow to God, but only 'after vows is he disposed to make examination.' (Proverbs 20:25) Would it not, then, make sense to examine yourself in the light of the

Scriptures *before* you enter into something as serious as a vow of marriage? Just what are your goals in life? How will these be affected by marriage? Do you want to get married simply to experience sexual relations or to escape problems?

Also, to what extent are you prepared to take on the role of husband or wife? Are you capable of managing a household or making a living? If you find yourself in constant conflict with your parents, will you be able to get along with a marriage mate? Can you withstand the trials and tribulations that come with marriage? Have you truly put away "the traits of a babe" when it comes to handling money? (1 Corinthians 13:11) Your parents will no doubt have much to say as to how you measure up.

Marriage can be a source of rich happiness or of most bitter pain. Much depends upon how ready you are for it. If you are still a teenager, why not wait a while before you begin dating? Waiting will not harm you. It will simply give you the time you need to be truly ready if and when you take that serious—and permanent—step of marriage.

Questions for Discussion   Chapter 30

☐ *What immature views of marriage do some youths nurture?*

☐ *Why do you think it is unrealistic to marry just for sex?*

☐ *How have some youths proved to be unprepared for the role of husband or of wife?*

☐ *Why do young couples often have serious problems over money?*

☐ *What mistake do some youths make in selecting a marriage mate?*

☐ *What questions might you ask yourself regarding your readiness for marriage? After considering this information, how ready to undertake marriage do you feel you are?*

Chapter 31

How Do I Know If It's Real Love?

LOVE—to starry-eyed romantics it is a mysterious visitation that seizes you, a once-in-a-lifetime feeling of sheer ecstasy. Love, they believe, is strictly an affair of the heart, something that cannot be understood, just experienced. Love conquers all and lasts forever . . .

So go the romantic clichés. And no doubt about it, falling in love can be a uniquely beautiful experience. But just what is real love?

Love at First Sight?

David met Janet for the first time at a party. He was immediately attracted to her shapely figure and the way her hair tumbled over her eye when she laughed. Janet was enchanted by his deep brown eyes and his witty conversation. It seemed like a case of mutual love at first sight!

During the next three weeks, David and Janet were inseparable. Then one night Janet received a devastating phone call from a former boyfriend. She called David for comfort. But David, feeling threatened and confused, responded coldly. The love they thought would last forever died that night.

Is it the person you are in love with or just an "image"?

Movies, books, and television shows would have you believe that love at first sight lasts forever. Granted, physical attractiveness is usually what makes two people notice each other in the first place. As one young man put it: "It is hard to 'see' a person's personality." But what is it that one "loves" when a relationship is but a few hours or days old? Is it not the image that person projects? Really, you don't know much about that person's thoughts, hopes, fears, plans, habits, skills, or abilities. You've met only the outer shell, not "the secret person of the heart." (1 Peter 3:4) How enduring could such love be?

Looks Are Deceiving

Furthermore, outward appearances can be deceiving. The Bible says: "Charm may be false, and prettiness may be vain." The glittering wrappings of a gift tell you nothing of what's inside. In fact, the most elegant wrappings may cover a useless gift.—Proverbs 31:30.

The Proverbs say: "As a gold nose ring in the snout of a pig, so is a woman that is pretty but that is turning away from sensibleness." (Proverbs 11:22) Nose rings were a popular adornment during Bible times. They were exquisite, often made of solid gold. Naturally, such a ring would be the first piece of jewelry you would notice on a woman.

Appropriately, the proverb compares an outwardly beautiful woman who lacks "sensibleness" to a "nose ring in the snout of a pig." Beauty simply does not befit

a senseless woman; it is a useless ornament on her. In the long run, it no more makes her appealing than would a gorgeous nose ring beautify a pig! What a mistake it is, then, to fall 'in love' with the way someone looks—and ignore what that person is inside.

"The Most Deceitful Thing There Is"

Some, however, feel that the human heart has infallible romantic judgment. 'Just listen to your heart,' they argue. 'You will know when it's real love!' Unfortunately, the facts contradict this notion. A survey was taken in which 1,079 young people (ages 18 to 24) reported having experienced an average of seven romantic involvements up to that time. Most admitted that their past romances were mere infatuation—a passing, fading emotion. Yet, these youths "invariably described their current experience as love"! Most, though, will likely one day view their current involvements as they did their past ones—as mere infatuations.

The tragedy is that thousands of couples every year marry under the illusion of being 'in love,' only to find shortly thereafter that they have seriously erred. Infatuation "lures unsuspecting men and women into poor marriages like lambs to the slaughter," says Ray Short in his book *Sex, Love, or Infatuation.*

"He that is trusting in his own heart is stupid." (Proverbs 28:26) Far too often, the judgment of our

A physically attractive, but senseless, man or woman is 'like a gold ring in the snout of a pig'

*I*s It Love or Infatuation?

LOVE	INFATUATION
1. An unselfish caring about the interests of the other	**1.** Is selfish, restrictive. One thinks, 'What does this do for me?'
2. Romance often starts slowly, perhaps taking months or years	**2.** Romance starts fast, perhaps taking hours or days
3. You are attracted by the other person's total personality and spiritual qualities	**3.** You are deeply impressed or interested in the other's physical appearance. ('He has such dreamy eyes.' 'She's got a great figure')
4. The effect on you is that it makes you a better person	**4.** A destructive, disorganizing effect
5. You view the other realistically, seeing his or her faults, yet loving that one anyway	**5.** Is unrealistic. The other person seems perfect. You ignore any nagging doubts about serious personality flaws
6. You have disagreements, but you find that you can talk them out and settle them	**6.** Arguments are frequent. Nothing really gets settled. Many are "settled" with a kiss
7. You want to give and share with the other person	**7.** The emphasis is on taking or getting, especially in satisfying sexual urges

heart is misguided or misdirected. In fact, the Bible says: "The heart is the most deceitful thing there is." (Jeremiah 17:9, *The Living Bible*) Yet, the aforementioned proverb continues: "But he that is walking in wisdom is the one that will escape." You too can escape the dangers and frustrations other youths have suffered if you learn the difference between infatuation and the love described in the Bible—the love that never fails.

Love Versus Infatuation

"Infatuation is blind and it likes to stay that way. It doesn't like to look at reality," admits 24-year-old Calvin. A 16-year-old girl, Kenya, added, "When you're infatuated with a person, you think that everything they do is just perfect."

Infatuation is counterfeit love. It is unrealistic and self-centered. Infatuated persons have a tendency to say: 'I really feel important when I'm with him. I can't sleep. I can't believe how fantastic this is' or, 'She really makes me feel good.' Notice how many times either "I" or "me" is used? A relationship based on selfishness is bound to fail! Note, however, the Bible's description of true love: "Love is long-suffering and kind. Love is not jealous, it does not brag, does not get puffed up, does not behave indecently, does not look for its own interests, does not become provoked. It does not keep account of the injury."—1 Corinthians 13:4, 5.

Since it "does not look for its own interests," love based on Bible principle is neither self-centered nor selfish. True, a couple may have strong romantic feelings and mutual attraction. But these feelings are balanced by reason and deep respect for the other person.

A person who constantly puts you down before others may well lack genuine love for you

ation for your feelings. These are hardly desirable qualities in a marriage mate.

What if the breakup is entirely one-sided and you are convinced that a marriage would have worked out well? Certainly you have a right to let the other person know how you feel. Perhaps there have simply been some misunderstandings. Emotional ranting and raving accomplishes little. And if he or she insists on splitting up, there is no need for you to humiliate yourself, tearfully begging for the affections of someone who obviously has no feelings for you. Solomon said there is "a time to seek and a time to give up as lost."—Ecclesiastes 3:6.

What if you have strong reason to suspect that you were merely being used by someone who never had a sincere interest in marriage in the first place? You need not resort to vindictive reprisals. Be assured that his or her deviousness is

not unnoticed by God. His Word says: "The cruel person is bringing ostracism upon his own organism."—Proverbs 11:17; compare Proverbs 6:12-15.

From time to time you may still be tormented by loneliness or romantic memories. If so, it's all right to have a good cry. It also helps to get busy, perhaps in some physical activity or the Christian ministry. (Proverbs 18:1) Keep your mind on things that are cheerful and upbuilding. (Philippians 4:8) Confide in a close friend. (Proverbs 18:24) Your parents may also be of great comfort, even if you feel you are old enough to be independent. (Proverbs 23:22) And above all, confide in Jehovah.

You may now see the need to work on certain aspects of your personality. Your vision of what you want in a marriage mate may be clearer than ever. And having loved and lost, you may decide to handle courtship a bit more prudently should a desirable person come along again—the likelihood of which may be greater than you think.

It Takes Time!

True love is therefore not hurt by time. Indeed, often the best way to test out your feelings for someone is to let some time pass. Furthermore, as a young woman named Sandra observed: "A person just doesn't hand out to you his personality by simply saying: 'This is what I am. Now you know all about me.'" No, it also takes time to get to know someone you are interested in.

> **"I can only be a 'Hi, how are you?' person now. I am not letting any person get close to me"**

Time also allows you to examine your romantic interest in the light of the Bible. Remember, love "does not behave indecently, does not look for its own interests." Is your companion eager for the success of your plans—or only for his or her own? Does he or she show respect for your viewpoint, your feelings? Has he or she pressured you to do things that are really 'indecent' in order to satisfy selfish passions? Does this person tend to put you down or build you up in front of others? Asking questions like these can help you appraise your feelings more objectively.

Rushing romance invites disaster. "I just fell in love, fast and deep," explained 20-year-old Jill. After a whirlwind romance of two months, she married. But previously concealed faults began to emerge. Jill began to display some of her insecurity and self-centeredness. Her husband, Rick, lost his romantic charm and became selfish. After being married for about two years, Jill one day screamed that her husband was "cheap," "lazy," and a "flop" as a husband. Rick responded by striking her in the face with his fist. In tears, Jill dashed out of their house—and out of their marriage.

Following the Bible's counsel would no doubt have

*O*bserving each other in a group can allow you to become acquainted without romantic involvement

also helps to find out what kind of reputation he or she has by talking with someone who knows the person well.—Compare Proverbs 31:31.

The First Dates

Having decided that someone might be a suitable marriage mate for you, you could approach the person and express a desire to get to know that one better.* Assuming there is a positive response, your first date need not be some elaborate affair. Perhaps a lunch date or even being part of a group date will enable you to become better acquainted so as to decide whether you want to take the relationship any further. Keeping things somewhat informal helps ease some of the nervousness both might feel initially. And by avoiding premature expressions of commitment, you can minimize feelings of rejection—or embarrassment—if one of you loses interest.

Regardless of the type of date planned, show up on time, neatly and appropriately dressed. Display the skills of a good conversationalist. Be an active listener.

---

* This applies in lands where dating is customary and is viewed as appropriate conduct for Christians. Usually the male takes the initiative, though there is no Scriptural principle that would prevent a young woman from expressing her feelings in a modest way if a young man seems shy or hesitant.—Compare Song of Solomon 8:6.

(James 1:19) Though there are no hard-and-fast rules in such matters, a young man will want to follow local rules of etiquette. These may include opening a door for the young lady or helping her into her seat. A young woman, while not expecting to be treated like a princess, should cooperate modestly with her date's efforts. By treating each other with mutual respect, a couple can set a pattern for the future. A husband is commanded to 'honor his wife as the weaker vessel.' And a wife is to have "deep respect for her husband."—1 Peter 3:7; Ephesians 5:33.

Is holding hands, kissing, or embracing appropriate, and if so, when? Displays of affection, when performed as genuine expressions of endearment and not selfish passion, can be both clean and appropriate. The Bible book The Song of Solomon indicates that some fitting expressions of endearment had been exchanged between the Shulammite maiden and the shepherd boy she loved and would soon marry. (Song of Solomon 1:2; 2:6; 8:5) But as with that chaste pair, a couple would further take care that displays of affection do not become unclean or lead to sexual immorality.* (Galatians 5:19, 21) Logically, such expressions of endearment should be made only when the relationship has

---

* See Chapter 24, "How Can I Say No to Premarital Sex?"

*O*beying local rules of etiquette and good manners sets a pattern of mutual respect that can carry over into marriage

reached a point where mutual commitment has developed and marriage seems imminent. By showing self-control, you can avoid being distracted from a primary aim of successful courtship, namely . . .

Getting to Know "the Secret Person of the Heart"

A research team reported in the May 1980 issue of the *Journal of Marriage and the Family:* "Marriages seem more likely to survive and prosper if people enter them with relatively full knowledge of one another's inner selves." Yes, getting to know "the secret person of the heart" of your partner is essential.—1 Peter 3:4.

Yet, 'drawing up' the intentions of the heart of another takes effort and discernment. (Proverbs 20:5) So plan activities

> *"Marriages seem more likely to survive and prosper if people enter them with relatively full knowledge of one another's inner selves."—Journal of Marriage and the Family*

that are more likely to help you see your partner's inner self. While going to a movie or a concert may suffice at the start, engaging in activities that better lend themselves to conversation (such as roller-skating, bowling, and visiting zoos, museums, and art galleries) can do more to help you become better acquainted.

To get a glimpse of your partner's feelings, try using open-ended questions, such as, 'How do you spend your free time?' 'If money were no object, what would you like to do?' 'What feature of our worship of God do you like the best? Why?' These allow in-depth responses that help you learn what your partner treasures.

As the relationship deepens and the two of you more seriously consider marriage, there is need for serious

Should We Break Up?

As a romance approaches the crossroads of decision, it is not unusual for doubts to arise. What if such doubts stem from serious flaws in the person you are dating or from flaws in the relationship itself?

For example, it is true that even people who love each other can disagree at times. (Compare Genesis 30:2; Acts 15:39.) But if you disagree on just about everything, if every discussion turns into a shouting match, or if your relationship is a never-ending cycle of breakups and makeups, beware! A poll of 400 physicians revealed that constant bickering is a strong indicator of "emotional unreadiness for marriage," perhaps even revealing "irreconcilable conflict between the couple."

Another cause for concern may be your discovery of disturbing personality flaws in a prospective mate. A display of a violent temper or even hints of selfishness, immaturity, moodiness, or stubbornness may make you wonder if you want to spend the rest of your life with this person. Yet many overlook or try to justify such shortcomings and seem determined to make the relationship work at all costs. Why is this?

Since courtship is taken seriously among true Christians—as well it should be—some feel pressured to marry the person they are dating. They may also dread having to confront and perhaps hurt this person. Others may simply fear that they will not be able to find someone else to marry. Nevertheless, these are not good reasons for prolonging a problem-plagued courtship.

The purpose of courtship is to investigate the possibility of marriage. And if a Christian starts a courtship in good faith, he or she has no obligation to continue it if it proves faulty. Besides, would it not be wrong and selfish to prolong a deteriorating relationship on the premise, 'maybe I won't find someone

else?' (Compare Philippians 2:4.) It is thus important that you face—not evade—your problems as a couple. Begin by taking a hard look at the person you are dating.

For example, is there evidence that this is a woman who will be a submissive, capable wife? (Proverbs 31: 10-31) Is there evidence this is a man who will show self-sacrificing love and be an able provider? (Ephesians 5: 28, 29; 1 Timothy 5:8) A person may claim to be a zealous servant of God, but are there works to back up such a claim of faith? —James 2:17, 18.

Of course, if you have invested much time and emotion in developing a relationship, do not be quick to call it off just because you have discovered that he or she is not perfect. (James 3:2) Perhaps the per-

son's flaws are ones you can live with.

What if they are not? Talk matters over. Do you have fundamental differences in goals or viewpoints? Or have there simply been misunderstandings? Could it be a case of both of you needing to learn how to 'restrain your spirit' and settle matters more calmly? (Proverbs 25: 28) If irritating personality quirks concern you, does he or she humbly admit the shortcomings and show a desire to improve? Is there a need on your part to be less sensitive, less touchy? (Ecclesiastes 7:9) 'Putting up with each other in love' is the lifeblood of a good marriage. —Ephesians 4:2.

Far from destroying your relationship, talking matters out may well reveal the potential it has for future growth! But if the discussion simply results in another frustrating standoff, do not ignore clear signs of impending disaster. (Proverbs 22:3) Things are not likely to improve after marriage. Calling the courtship off may be in the best interests of both of you.

talk about important issues such as your values; where and how you will live; financial matters, including whether both will work outside the home; children; birth control; concepts of each one's role in marriage; and both immediate and long-range goals and how you plan to achieve these. Many young Witnesses of Jehovah become full-time evangelizers after finishing school and desire to continue serving in that way after marriage. Now is the time for the two of you to make sure your spiritual goals are compatible. It is also a time to reveal things, perhaps in your past, that may affect the marriage. These might include any major debts or obligations. Health matters, such as any serious disease, and their consequences should also be frankly discussed.

In such discussions, follow the example of Elihu, who said: "I talk straight from my heart and speak sincerely." (Job 33:3, *The Holy Bible in the Language of Today,* by William Beck) In explaining how her courtship prepared her for what proved to be a happy marriage, Esther said: "I never tried to 'put on' or say I agreed with Jaye when I felt differently. I still don't. I try always to be honest."

Do not evade or gloss over sensitive subjects out of fear of putting your partner on the spot. Beth made this mistake during her courtship with John. Beth said she believed in saving for the future and not wasting money. John said he agreed. Beth probed no further, imagining they saw eye to eye on matters of finance. But it turned out that John's idea of saving for the future meant saving for a new sports car! After marriage their lack of agreement on how to spend money became painfully evident.

Such misunderstandings can be prevented. Louise, mentioned previously, says in retrospect of her courtship: "I should have asked a lot more questions, such as,

YOUNG PEOPLE ASK . . .

When it becomes apparent that a courtship is not working out, the kind thing to do is to have a face-to-face discussion, explaining why the relationship must end

'What if I got pregnant and you didn't want to have a baby, what would you do?' Or, 'If we were in debt and I wanted to stay home and care for our child, how would you handle matters?' I would have carefully noted his reaction." Such discussions can bring to the surface qualities of the heart that should best be seen before marriage.

See Him or Her in Action!

"A person can be very nice with you on a one-to-one basis," explained Esther. "But when others are around, they are often put into an unexpected situation. One of your friends might say something to your partner that he might not like. Now you get to see how he reacts under pressure. Will he tell the person off or be sarcastic?" She concludes: "Being around each other's friends and family during our courtship helped tremendously."

In addition to recreation, spend time working together. Share in Christian works, including the study of God's Word and the Christian ministry. Also, take on some of the daily chores that after marriage will become a way of life—shopping for food, preparing a meal, washing dishes, and housecleaning. By being together under real-life circumstances—when your partner may even be at his or her worst—you can see behind any display-window mask.

The shepherd boy of The Song of Solomon saw how

the girl he loved acted when she was disappointed or while she was laboring under the scorching sun —sweaty and tired. (Song of Solomon 1:5, 6; 2:15) After also beholding how she loyally resisted the enticements of rich King Solomon, he exclaimed: "You are altogether beautiful, O girl companion of mine, and there is no defect in you." (Song of Solomon 4:7) Surely he did not mean that she was perfect, but that she had no basic moral defect or blemish. Her physical beauty was enhanced by her moral strength, which outweighed any weaknesses on her part.—Compare Job 31:7.

To make a similar assessment takes time. So avoid a hasty courtship. (Proverbs 21:5) Usually a man and woman will go all out to win each other's love. But if given enough time, unpleasant habits and tendencies have a way of revealing themselves. A couple who not only take time but also make the best use of it during courtship will likely find an easier adjustment after marriage. With eyes wide open, they can enter marriage confident of being able to work out disagreements that will arise. Successful courtship has prepared them for a successful and happy marriage.

Questions for Discussion   Chapter 32

☐ *What is a primary aim of courtship, and how important is it to marital happiness?*

☐ *What will help you get to know another's 'inner self'?*

☐ *What kind of conversations contribute to a successful courtship?*

☐ *Why is spending time together under a variety of circumstances helpful?*

☐ *What are some indicators that a relationship is faulty?*

☐ *When should a courtship be called off?*

The Trap of Drugs and Alcohol

Marijuana, cocaine, crack, booze. These have become as much a part of some teenagers' lives as rock music. But regardless of what your peers may tell you, drugs and alcohol are a lethal trap. Why have alarming numbers of youths fallen into it? And what can you do to avoid falling in yourself?

Chapter 33

Drinking—Why Not?

'IS IT wrong to drink? Is it really harmful? Or is it wrong only for me but all right for adults?' These questions may very well go through your mind. After all, your parents may indulge. Many young people your age (legal age limits notwithstanding) are drinking. TV shows and movies make it look appealing.

When used moderately, alcohol can indeed be a source of pleasure. The Bible acknowledges that wine can make the heart merry or can enhance the taste of a meal. (Ecclesiastes 9:7) When misused, however, alcohol creates serious problems ranging from run-ins with parents, teachers, and police to premature death. As the Bible says: "Wine is a ridiculer, intoxicating liquor is boisterous, and everyone going astray by it is not wise." (Proverbs 20:1) It is important, then, that you make a responsible decision about drinking.

Peers, television, and sometimes even parents can influence youths to begin drinking

But how much do you really know about alcohol and its effects? The following test will enable you to find out. Simply mark the following True or False:

1. *Alcoholic beverages are predominantly stimulants* .... —

2. *Alcohol in any quantity is damaging to the human body* .... —

3. *All alcoholic beverages—liquor, wine, beer—are absorbed into your bloodstream at the same rate* ... —

4. *A person can sober up more quickly if he drinks black coffee or takes a cold shower* .... —

5. *Alcohol in the same amount has the same effect on everybody who drinks* .... —

6. *Drunkenness is the same as alcoholism* .... —

7. *Alcohol and other sedative drugs (such as barbiturates) when taken together multiply each other's effects* .... —

8. *Switching drinks will keep a person from getting drunk* .... —

9. *The body digests alcohol just like food* .... —

Now check your answers against those given on page 270. Did some of your views on alcohol prove wrong? If so, realize that ignorance regarding alcohol can be deadly. The Bible warns us that improperly used, alcohol "bites just like a serpent, and it secretes poison just like a viper."—Proverbs 23:32.

John, for example, married as a teenager. One night, after a fight with his young wife, he stormed out of the house, determined to get drunk. After gulping down a whole pint of vodka, he fell into a coma. Were it not for the efforts of doctors and nurses, John could have died. Evidently he didn't realize that rapidly gulping down a large amount of alcohol can even be fatal. Ignorance almost cost him his life.

'Why We Started Drinking'

An interview with some former teenage drinkers

Interviewer: Why did you drink?

Bill: For me, at first it was the group I was in. It was the "in" thing to do, especially on weekends.

Dennis: I started drinking at about age 14 or so. My father was a pretty heavy drinker. There were always cocktail parties at the house. As a child I saw that drinking was the thing to do socially. Then, when I got older, I got in with a wild crowd. I used to drink to be accepted by the other kids.

Mark: I was involved in sports. I guess I started drinking at about age 15 with the guys on the basketball team. It was mainly, I think, curiosity.

Joan: I was affected very much by what I saw on TV. I used to see the characters drinking. It looked so great.

Paul: My father is an alcoholic. Now I can see that the reason we had so many problems was the alcoholism. I was trying to escape from it. Ironically, that's one reason I turned to drinking.

Joan: My parents usually didn't drink much. But I remember one thing about my dad, on social occasions he used to brag about how much he could drink. I kind of developed that attitude —thinking I was unique. One time my friends and I went on a drinking binge. For hours we were drinking. It really didn't affect me like the others. I remember thinking, 'I'm just like my dad.' I guess his attitude about alcohol really did affect me.

Interviewer: But why do many drink to the point of intoxication?

Mark: That's the reason we drank—to get drunk. I really didn't care for the taste.

Interviewer: So you drank for the effect?

Mark: Yes.

Harry: I'd say the same thing. It's like climbing a ladder. Each time you drink you're reaching for a better high—the next rung on the ladder.

The Rebound Effect

This is one of alcohol's most insidious effects. Alcohol is a depressant, not a stimulant. The seeming uplift you feel after you drink occurs because alcohol depresses, or brings down, your anxiety level. You feel relaxed, less anxious, less worried than before you drank. Taken in moderate quantities, alcohol can thus, to a small extent, help a person 'forget his troubles.' (Proverbs 31: 6, 7) A youth named Paul, for instance, drank to escape from family problems. "I learned very early that drinking was a way to relieve the pressure I was under," he recalls. "It relaxed my mind."

No harm done, right? Wrong! Alcohol has a rebound effect. After a couple of hours, when the sedative effect of the alcohol wears off, your anxiety level bounces back —but not back to normal. It jumps up to a higher level than before you drank! You feel more anxious or more tense than ever. Alcohol withdrawal may last for up to 12 hours. True, if you have another drink, your anxiety level will again go down. But a couple of hours later, it will rise, this time higher than before! And so it goes in a vicious spiral of artificial highs and ever-lower lows.

So in the long run, alcohol will not really reduce your anxiety. It may very well increase it. And when the alcohol wears off, your problems are still there.

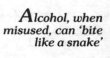

Alcohol, when misused, can 'bite like a snake'

Driving and Drinking—A Deadly Combination

"Drunk driving is the leading cause of death for young people aged 16-24," says the 1984 Report on the National Conference for Youth on Drinking and Driving. Indeed, "a teenager is four times more likely to have an alcohol-related crash than any other driver." (Just Along for the Ride) Such needless carnage is in part due to the persistence of many myths about the effects of alcohol. Here are a few typical examples:

MYTH: It's safe to drive if all you've had is a couple of beers.

FACT: "The alcohol in two 12-ounce cans of beer consumed in less than an hour can slow a driver's reaction by 2/5ths of a second—allowing an automobile traveling at 55 miles per hour to travel an additional 34 feet—possibly the difference between a near miss and a crash."—Development of a Traffic Safety and Alcohol Program for Senior Adults, by James L. Malfetti, Ed.D., and Darlene J. Winter, Ph.D.

MYTH: It's OK to drive as long as you don't feel drunk.

FACT: It's dangerous to rely on how you feel. Alcohol creates an illusion of well-being, making the drinker feel that he's in control, when in fact his abilities have been diminished.

Dangerous as it is for anyone to mix drinking and driving, it's even riskier for youths. The driving performance of youths who are drinking "worsens more rapidly than that of adults because driving is a newer and less routine skill for them. In short, most teenagers are both inexperienced drivers and inexperienced drinkers, and even more inexperienced at combining drinking and driving."—Senior Adults, Traffic Safety and Alcohol Program Leader's Guide, by Darlene J. Winter, Ph.D.

It also takes less alcohol to intoxicate a youth than an adult. Youths generally weigh less than adults, and the less a person weighs, the less fluid there is in his body to dilute the alcohol he consumes. The higher the concentration of alcohol in your bloodstream, the more intoxicated you become.

"Shrewd is the one that has seen the calamity and proceeds to conceal himself, but the inexperienced have passed along and must suffer the penalty." (Proverbs 22:3) Given the dangers of mixing drinking and driving, you are "shrewd" if you promise yourself not to mix the two. You can thus not only spare yourself crippling—or fatal—injuries but also show respect for the lives of others.

You should further resolve that you will (1) never get in a car with a driver who's been drinking and (2) never let a friend drive if he's been drinking. This may upset your friend, but he may appreciate what you did once he comes to his senses.—Compare Psalm 141:5.

Never get in a car with a driver who's been drinking, and never let a friend drive if he's been drinking

Emotionally Stunted

Others claim that alcohol helps them to function better. Dennis, for example, was extremely shy and found it difficult to hold even a simple conversation. But then he made a discovery. "After a few drinks I would loosen up," he said.

The problem is that one matures, not by running from difficult situations, as Dennis did, but by facing them. Learning to cope with the problems you face as a youth is just a rehearsal for the trials of adulthood.

Drinking can trap a young person in a vicious spiral of artificial highs and ever-lower lows

Dennis thus found that, in the long run, the temporary effects of alcohol did not help him to overcome his shyness. "When the alcohol wore off, I went back into my shell," he reports. What about now, years later? Dennis continues: "I never really learned how to communicate with people on my own true level. I think I was stunted in this way."

The same is true of using alcohol as a crutch in dealing with stress. Joan, who did so as a teenager, admits: "Recently, in a stressful situation I thought: 'It would be nice to have a *drink* right now.' You think that you can handle a situation better with a drink." Not so!

An article published in the *New York State Journal of Medicine* says: "When drugs [including alcohol] become the means of easing difficult situations—academic, social, or interpersonal—the necessity for learning healthy coping skills is removed. Effects may not be felt until adulthood, when establishing close personal relationships then often proves difficult, leaving the individual emotionally isolated." It is far better to meet and deal with problems and difficult situations directly!

Drinking and driving often leads to this

"He Would Not Take It"

Consider the example of Jesus Christ. On the final night of his earthly life, Jesus endured a terribly stressful ordeal. Betrayed, then arrested, Jesus endured a series of interrogations in which lying accusations were made against him. Finally, after having been up all night, he was handed over to be impaled.—Mark 14: 43–15:15; Luke 22:47–23:25.

Jesus was then offered something that would dull his senses—a mood-altering substance that would make it easier for him to cope with this difficult situation. The Bible explains: "They tried to give him wine drugged with myrrh, but he would not take it." (Mark 15:22, 23) Jesus wanted to be in possession of all his faculties. He wanted to face this difficult situation squarely. He was no escapist! Later, though, when offered evidently a moderate amount of *undrugged* wine to quench his thirst, Jesus accepted.—John 19:28-30.

In comparison, your problems, pressures, or stresses pale into insignificance. But you can still learn a valuable lesson from Jesus' experience. Instead of using

*A*nswers to True or False Test   (Page 263)

1. FALSE. *Alcohol is predominantly a depressant. It can make you high in that it depresses, or reduces, your anxiety level, making you feel relaxed, less anxious than before you drank.*

2. FALSE. *Drinking moderate or small amounts of alcohol does not appear to do any serious harm to the body. However, prolonged and heavy drinking can damage the heart, brain, liver, and other organs.*

3. FALSE. *Liquor or spirits are generally absorbed faster than wine or beer.*

4. FALSE. *Coffee can wake you up, and a cold shower can make you wet, but alcohol continues in your bloodstream until it is metabolized by your liver at the rate of about one half ounce of alcohol per hour.*

5. FALSE. *A number of factors, such as your body weight and whether you've eaten or not, can influence how alcohol affects you.*

6. FALSE. *Drunkenness describes the result of overconsumption. Alcoholism is characterized by a loss of control over drinking. However, not everyone who gets drunk is an alcoholic, and not all alcoholics get drunk.*

7. TRUE. *When mixed with alcohol, some drugs greatly exaggerate the usual reactions expected from alcohol or from the drug alone. For example, mixing alcohol and tranquilizers or sedatives could result in severe withdrawal symptoms, coma, and even death. Thus, one drink plus one pill has a far greater effect than you might imagine. Indeed, the effect of the drug is multiplied three times, four times, ten times, or even more!*

8. FALSE. *Drunkenness is a result of the total amount of alcohol consumed, whether it's in gin, whiskey, vodka, or whatever.*

9. FALSE. *Alcohol doesn't have to be digested slowly the way most other foods must be. Rather, about 20 percent immediately passes through the walls of the stomach into the bloodstream. The rest goes from the stomach to the small intestine, and from there it is absorbed into the bloodstream.*

a mood-altering substance (such as alcohol) to cope with problems, pressures, and uncomfortable situations, you are much better off if you deal with them directly. The more experience you gain in facing life's problems, the better you will become at solving them. You will grow to have a healthy emotional makeup.

"I never really learned how to communicate with people on my own true level. I think I was stunted in this way."—A young man who abused alcohol as a teenager

When you come of legal age, whether or not you choose to drink occasionally—and in moderation—will be a decision for you (and perhaps your parents) to make. Let it be an informed decision, an intelligent decision. If you choose not to drink, you have nothing to apologize about. But if you're of legal age and decide to drink, drink responsibly. Never drink as an escape or in order to gain artificial courage. The Bible's advice is simple and straightforward: "Drinking too much makes you loud and foolish. It's stupid to get drunk."—Proverbs 20:1, *Today's English Version*.

Questions for Discussion   Chapter 33

☐ *Why do many youths become involved in drinking alcoholic beverages?*

☐ *What are some common misconceptions about alcohol?*

☐ *What are the dangers in mixing driving and drinking?*

☐ *What are the dangers of using alcohol in order to escape from problems?*

☐ *What should a youth do when he encounters problems, and why?*

Chapter 34

Why Say *No* to Drugs?

"I AM an emotional child," says Mike, a young man 24 years old. "At times I'm afraid and even intimidated by others my own age. I suffer from depression, insecurity, and at times I've even considered suicide."

Ann, 36 years old, describes herself as "emotionally very young," having "low self-esteem." She adds: "I find it very difficult to live a normal life."

Mike and Ann are reaping the consequences of a decision they made when they were quite young, that is, to experiment with drugs. Millions of youths today are doing likewise—injecting, swallowing, sniffing, and smoking everything from cocaine to marijuana. For some youths, 'doing drugs' is a way to escape problems. Others get involved to satisfy their curiosity. Yet others use drugs to ease depression or boredom. And once started, many continue using drugs for the sheer pleasure of it. Says 17-year-old Grant: "I smoke [marijuana] only for its effects. Not to be cool or for social reasons. . . . I never smoked because of peer pressure, but just because I wanted to."

At any rate, the chances are good that sooner or later you will be exposed to or directly offered drugs. "Even the guards at our school are selling pot [marijuana]," says one youth. Drug paraphernalia is openly displayed and sold. In spite of their popularity, though, there is good reason for you to say *no* to drugs. How so?

Drugs Hinder Growth

Consider youths who use drugs to escape problems, like Mike and Ann. As was shown in our previous chap-

YOUNG PEOPLE ASK . . .

ter, emotional growth comes from facing life's challenges, handling success, surviving failure. Youths who rely on a chemical refuge from problems hinder their emotional development. They fail to develop the skills needed for coping with problems.

As with any other skill, the ability to cope requires practice. To illustrate: Have you ever watched a skilled soccer player? He is able to use his head and feet in ways that are nothing short of amazing! Yet, how did this player develop such skill? By years of practice. He learned to kick the ball, run with it, feint, and so on, until he became proficient at the game.

Developing coping skills is very similar. It takes practice—experience! Yet, at Proverbs 1:22 the Bible asks: "How long will you inexperienced ones keep loving inexperience, . . . and how long will you stupid ones keep hating knowledge?" The youth that hides behind a drug-induced euphoria 'loves inexperience'; he fails to develop the knowledge and coping skills needed to deal with life. As the book *Talking With Your Teenager* says of teenage drug users: "The lesson that life's painful moments can be survived without these substances never gets learned."

Ann, who used drugs as an escape, thus confesses:

"For 14 years I haven't dealt with my problems." Mike expressed a similar thought, saying: "I had used drugs since I was 11 years old. When I stopped at the age of 22, I felt like a child. I latched onto others, trying to find security. I came to realize that my emotional development stopped when I started using drugs."

> "*Even the guards at our school are selling pot,*" says one youth

"I wasted all those years of development," adds Frank, who abused drugs from age 13. "When I stopped, I came to the painful realization that I was totally unprepared to deal with life. I was a 13-year-old all over again with the same emotional turmoil that faces any other adolescent."

Can Drugs Ruin My Health?

This is another area of concern. Most youths realize that the so-called hard drugs can kill you. But what about so-called soft drugs, such as marijuana? Are all the warnings you hear about them mere scare tactics? In answer, let us focus on the drug marijuana.

Marijuana (also known as pot, reefer, grass, ganja, or weed) has been the focus of much controversy among experts. And admittedly, much is unknown regarding this popular drug. For one thing, marijuana is extremely complex; a marijuana cigarette contains over 400 chemical compounds in its smoke. It took doctors over 60 years to realize cigarette smoke causes cancer. It may likewise take decades before anyone knows for sure just what marijuana's 400 compounds do to the human body.

Nevertheless, after studying thousands of research papers, a panel of experts of the prestigious U.S. Institute of Medicine concluded: "The scientific evidence published to date indicates that marijuana has a broad range of psychological and biological effects, some of which, at least under certain conditions, are harmful to human health." What are some of these harmful effects?

Marijuana—What It Does to Your Body

Consider, for example, the lungs. Even marijuana's staunchest supporters admit that inhaling smoke cannot possibly be good for you. Marijuana smoke, like the smoke from tobacco, consists of a number of toxic substances, such as tars.

Dr. Forest S. Tennant, Jr., surveyed 492 U.S. Army soldiers who had used marijuana. Nearly 25 percent of them "suffered sore throats from smoking cannabis, and some 6 percent reported that they had suffered from bronchitis." In another study, 24 out of 30 marijuana users were found to have bronchial "lesions characteristic of the early stages of cancer."

True, no one can guarantee that such ones will actually develop cancer later on. But would you want to run that risk? Besides, the Bible says that God "gives to all persons life and breath." (Acts 17:25) Would you be

Have the courage to say no to drugs!

Escape your problems through drugs now . . .

and you may find it hard to face problems as an adult

showing respect for the Giver of life if you deliberately inhaled something that damages the lungs and the throat?

At Ecclesiastes 12:6 the human brain is poetically called "the golden bowl." Barely larger than your fist and weighing a scant three pounds, the brain is not only the precious receptacle of your memories but also the command center for your entire nervous system. With that in mind, note the warning of the Institute of Medicine: "We can say with confidence that marijuana produces acute effects on the brain, including chemical and electrophysiological changes." At present, there is no conclusive proof that marijuana permanently damages the brain. Nevertheless, the possibility that marijuana might in any way do harm to "the golden bowl" should not be dismissed lightly.

And what about the prospect of your one day getting married and having children? The Institute of Medicine reported that marijuana is known "to cause birth defects when administered in large doses to experimental animals." Whether it has the same effects on humans is thus far unproved. Remember, though, that birth defects (such as the one caused by the hormone DES) often

276   *YOUNG PEOPLE ASK . . .*

take years to manifest themselves. So, what the future holds for the children—and grandchildren—of marijuana smokers remains to be seen. Dr. Gabriel Nahas says that smoking marijuana may be "genetic roulette." Could anyone who views children as "an inheritance from Jehovah" take such risks?—Psalm 127:3.

Drugs—The Bible's View

Of course, marijuana is just one of many popular drugs. But it well illustrates that there is ample reason to avoid taking any mind-altering substances for pleasure. Says the Bible: "The beauty of young men is their power." (Proverbs 20:29) As a young person, you no doubt enjoy good health. Why even risk throwing it away?

More important, though, we have the Bible's view on this matter. It tells us to "safeguard . . . thinking ability," not to ruin it through chemical abuse. (Proverbs 3:21) It further exhorts: "Let us cleanse ourselves of every defilement of flesh and spirit, perfecting holiness in God's fear." Really, it is only to those who have 'cleansed themselves of defilement,' avoiding practices like drug abuse, that God promises: "'I will take you in.' 'And I shall be a father to you.'"—2 Corinthians 6:17–7:1.

Nevertheless, turning down drugs may not be easy.

Marijuana—A New Wonder Drug?

There has been much ado over claims that marijuana may have therapeutic value in treating glaucoma and asthma and in easing the nausea that cancer patients experience during chemotherapy. A U.S. Institute of Medicine report acknowledges that there is some truth to these claims. But does this mean that in the near future doctors will be prescribing marijuana cigarettes?

Not likely, for while some of marijuana's over 400 chemical compounds may prove useful, smoking marijuana would hardly be the logical way to take such medicines.

"Using marijuana," says noted authority Dr. Carlton Turner, "would be like giving people molded bread to eat to get penicillin." So if any marijuana compounds ever become bona fide medicines, it will be marijuana "derivatives or analogues," chemical compounds similar to them, that doctors will prescribe. No wonder, then, that the U.S. Secretary of Health and Human Services wrote: "It should be emphasized that possible therapeutic benefits in no way modify the significance of the negative health effects of marijuana."

Peers and Their Pressure

One cool summer evening Joe and Frank, cousins and close friends, made a pact. "No matter what anyone else does," suggested Joe, the younger of the two, "let's never fool around with drugs." The two youths shook hands on the deal. Just five years later, Joe was found dead in his car as a result of a drug-related accident. And Frank was severely addicted to drugs.

What went wrong? The answer lies in this urgent warning found in the Bible: "Do not be misled. Bad associations spoil useful habits." (1 Corinthians 15:33) Joe and Frank both got in with the wrong crowd. As they associated more and more with those who used drugs, they began experimenting with drugs themselves.

The book *Self-Destructive Behavior in Children and Adolescents* observes: "The youthful are most often introduced or 'turned on' to the various drugs by a close friend . . . [His] intentions may be to share an exciting or pleasurable experience." Mike, mentioned at the outset, confirms this, saying: "Peer pressure to me was one of the hardest things to deal with. . . . The first time I smoked marijuana, I did it because all the kids I was with did it, and I wanted to fit in."

> *"I came to realize that my emotional development stopped when I started using drugs."*
> —Mike, a former drug user

To put it bluntly, if your friends start using drugs, you will be under strong emotional pressure to conform, to fit in. If you do not change your circle of friends, in all likelihood you will eventually become a drug user too.

"Walking With Wise Persons"

"He that is walking with wise persons will become wise, but he that is having dealings with the stupid ones will fare badly," says Proverbs 13:20. To illustrate the point, if you were trying to avoid catching a cold, would you not avoid close contact with infected people? "In a similar way," states the book *Adolescent Peer Pressure,* "if we are to prevent . . . drug abuse . . . , we need to maintain healthy balanced conditions and reduce exposure to harmful influences."

So do you want to say *no* to drugs? Then watch whom you associate with. Seek out the friendship of God-fearing Christians who will support your resolve to stay free of drugs. (Compare 1 Samuel 23:15, 16.) Note, too, the words at Exodus 23:2. Although originally directed to witnesses giving sworn testimony, they are good advice for youths: "You must not follow after the crowd for evil ends."

Someone who unquestioningly follows his peers is nothing more than a slave. Says the Bible at Romans 6:16 (*New International Version*): "Don't you know that when you offer yourselves to someone to obey him as slaves, you are slaves to the one whom you obey?" That is why the Bible encourages youths to develop "thinking ability." (Proverbs 2:10-12) Learn to think for yourself, and you'll not be inclined to follow wayward youths.

True, you may be curious about drugs and their effects. But you need not pollute your own mind and body to know what drugs do to people. Just observe drug abusers your age—especially those who have been abusers over a long period of time. Do they seem alert and sharp? Have they kept up their grades? Or are they dull and inattentive, at times even unaware of what is going on around them? A term was coined by drug users themselves to describe such ones: "burn-outs." Yet, many "burn-outs" likely started using drugs out of curiosity. No wonder, then, that the Bible urges Christians to suppress unhealthy curiosity and to "be babes as to badness."—1 Corinthians 14:20.

You Can Say No!

A booklet published by the U.S. National Institute on Drug Abuse reminds us: "Turning down the chance to use a drug . . . is your *right*. Any friends who lean on you about your decision are chipping away at your rights as a free individual." What can you do if someone offers you drugs? *Have the courage to say no!* This does not necessarily mean giving a sermon on the evils of drug abuse. The same booklet suggested simply replying, "No thanks, I don't want to smoke" or, "Nope, don't want the hassle" or even quipping, "I'm not into body pollution." If they persist in their offer, you might have to say *no,* with conviction! Letting others know that you are a Christian may also prove to be a protection.

Growing up is not easy. But if you try to avoid growing pains by using drugs, you can seriously hinder your chances of becoming a responsible, mature adult. Learn to face problems head-on. If the pressures seem overwhelming, do not seek a chemical escape. Talk things over with a parent or other responsible adults who can help you to sort things out. Remember, too, the Bible's exhortation: "Do not be anxious over anything, but in everything by prayer and supplication along with thanksgiving let your petitions be made known to God; and the peace of God that excels all thought will guard your hearts and your mental powers."—Philippians 4:6, 7.

Yes, Jehovah God will give you the strength to say *no!* Never let others pressure you to weaken in your resolve. As Mike urges: "Don't experiment with drugs. You'll suffer the rest of your life!"

Questions for Discussion   Chapter 34

□ *Why do so many youths become involved with drugs?*

□ *How can taking drugs hinder your emotional growth?*

□ *What is known about how marijuana affects the body?*

□ *What is the Bible's view of taking drugs for pleasure?*

□ *Why is watching your associations vital to remaining free from drugs?*

□ *What are some ways of saying no to drugs?*

Leisure Time

*I*n some developing countries, leisure time is a rare commodity. But in Western lands, youths often have more time on their hands than they know what to do with. Whether your leisure time is a blessing or a curse depends upon how you use it. In this section, we will look at some ways to use it productively.

Chapter 35

Does It Matter What I Read?

KING Solomon warned: "To the making of many books there is no end, and much devotion to them is wearisome to the flesh." (Ecclesiastes 12:12) Solomon was not trying to discourage reading; he was just advising you to be selective.

Seventeenth-century French philosopher René Descartes said: "When one reads good books it is like having a conversation with men of breeding who lived in the past. We might even call it a selective conversation in which the author expresses only his most noble thoughts." Not all writers, though, are worth 'conversing' with, nor are all their thoughts really "noble."

So the oft-quoted Bible principle again comes into play: "Bad associations spoil useful habits." (1 Corinthians 15:33) Yes, the people with whom you associate can mold your personality. Have you ever spent so much time with a friend that you found yourself

With so many thousands of books available, you must be selective

beginning to act, talk, and even think like your friend? Well, reading a book is like spending hours conversing with the one who wrote it.

The principle Jesus stated at Matthew 24:15 is thus pertinent: "Let the reader use discernment." Learn to analyze and weigh what you read. All humans are afflicted with a certain amount of bias and are not always totally honest in their portrayal of facts. Do not, therefore, accept unquestioningly everything you read or hear: "Anyone inexperienced puts faith in every word, but the shrewd one considers his steps."—Proverbs 14:15.

You should be particularly cautious about reading anything that expounds a philosophy of life. Teen magazines, for example, are full of advice on everything from dating to premarital sex—not always advice a Christian should use, however. And what about books that plunge into weighty philosophical questionings?

The Bible warns: "Look out: perhaps there may be someone who will carry you off as his prey through the philosophy and empty deception according to the tradition of men . . . and not according to Christ." (Colossians 2:8) The Bible, and Bible-based publications such as this, offer far better advice.—2 Timothy 3:16.

Romance Novels—Harmless Reading?

Reading romance novels has become an addictive habit for some 20 million people in the United States alone. Of course God himself placed in man and woman the desire to fall in love and marry. (Genesis 1:27, 28; 2:23, 24) It is no surprise, then, that romance is featured prominently in most fiction, and this is not necessarily objectionable. Some romance novels have even attained the status of fine literature. But since these older novels are considered tame by modern standards,

*R*omance novels may make absorbing reading, but do they teach a wholesome view of love and marriage?

writers have found it profitable of late to churn out a new breed of romance novels. Some still utilize historical or medieval settings to add drama and mood to the story. Others are contemporary in style and setting. Nevertheless, with a few minor variations, these modern romance novels follow a fairly predictable formula: heroes and heroines hurdling formidable obstacles that threaten their budding romance.

Typically, the hero is a strong, even arrogant, man who oozes self-confidence. The heroine, however, is likely to be delicate and vulnerable, often the hero's junior by 10 or 15 years. And though he often treats her contemptuously, she is still irresistibly attracted to him.

Often there is a rival suitor. Although he is kind and

considerate, he fails to excite or interest the heroine. So she uses her beguiling charms to mold her stoic hero into a tender soul who now openly declares his abiding love. All previous misgivings cleared and forgiven, they blissfully marry and live happily ever after . . .

Is Love Like the Love Stories?

Could reading such fanciful stories cloud your vision of reality? Bonnie, who started reading romance novels at age 16, recalls: "I looked for the young man that was tall, dark and handsome; one that was exciting, with a domineering personality." She confessed: "If I dated a young man and he didn't want to kiss and touch, he was dull, even though he was considerate and kind. I wanted the excitement I'd read about in the novels."

Bonnie continued to read romances after her marriage and says: "I had a nice home and family, but somehow it wasn't enough . . . I wanted the adventure, excitement and thrills so enticingly described in the novels. I felt something was wrong with my marriage." The Bible, though, helped Bonnie to appreciate that a husband must offer his wife more than charm or "excitement." It says: "Husbands ought to be loving their wives as their own bodies. He who loves his wife loves himself, for no man ever hated his own flesh; but he feeds and cherishes it." —Ephesians 5:28, 29.

And what about the themes so common to romance novels, the Utopian endings and the easy resolution of differences? Well, they are far from realistic. Bonnie recalls: "When I had a disagreement with my husband, instead of talking it out with him, I'd copy the gimmicks used by the heroine. When my husband didn't respond the way the hero did, I sulked." Is not the Bible's counsel for wives far more realistic and practical when it says, "You wives, be in subjection to your husbands"?—Colossians 3:18.

Sexual Content

Interestingly, sexually explicit romances—available in public libraries in some cities—are the ones most requested by teens. Can they harm you? Explains 18-year-old Karen: "The books really stirred strong sexual feelings and curiosity in me. The ecstasy and euphoric feelings felt by the heroine in passionate encounters with the hero caused me to desire those feelings too. So when I was dating," she continues, "I tried to recreate those sensations. It led me to commit fornication." But was her experience like those of the heroines she had read and fantasized about? Karen discovered: "These feelings are conjured up in the minds of the writers. They aren't real."

> *"I had a nice home and family, but somehow it wasn't enough ... I wanted the adventure, excitement and thrills so enticingly described in the novels. I felt something was wrong with my marriage"*

Creating sexual fantasies is indeed the intent of some authors. Consider the instructions one publisher gives to romance-novel authors: "Sexual encounters should concentrate on passion and the erotic sensations aroused by the hero's kisses and caresses." The writers are further advised that love stories "should evoke excitement, tension and a deep emotional and sensual response in the reader." Obviously, reading such material would not help one to follow the Bible's admonition to "deaden, therefore, your body members that are upon the earth as respects fornication, uncleanness, sexual appetite, hurtful desire."—Colossians 3:5.

Being Selective

It is best, then, to avoid novels that arouse immoral feelings or that engender unrealistic expectations. Why not branch out and try reading other types of books, such as history or science books? Not that fiction is off limits, for there are some fictional works that are not only entertaining but also educational. But if a novel features sex, senseless violence, occult practices, or "heroes" who are promiscuous, ruthless, or greedy, should you waste your time reading it?

So exercise care. Before reading a book, examine its cover and book jacket; see if there is anything objectionable about the book. And if in spite of precautions a book turns out to be unwholesome, have the strength of character to put the book down.

By way of contrast, reading the Bible and Bible-related publications will help, not harm, you. One Japanese girl, for example, says that reading the Bible helped her keep her mind off sex—often a problem for youths. "I always put the Bible near my bed and make a point of reading it before going to sleep," she says. "It is when I am alone and have nothing to do (such as at bedtime) that my mind sometimes turns toward sex. So reading the Bible really helps me!" Yes, "conversing" with the people of faith written about in the Bible can give you real moral fiber and greatly add to your happiness.—Romans 15:4.

Questions for Discussion	*Chapter 35*

☐ *Why must you be selective in what you read?*

☐ *Why are romance novels so appealing to many youths? But what are their dangers?*

☐ *How can you choose appropriate reading material?*

☐ *What are some of the benefits of reading the Bible and Bible-based publications?*

Chapter 36

How Can I Control My TV Viewing Habits?

FOR many, young and old, TV watching amounts to a serious addiction. Surveys indicate that by age 18 the average American youth will have watched some *15,000* hours of TV! And that a bona fide addiction is involved becomes obvious when hard-core viewers try to kick the habit.

"I find television almost irresistible. When the set is on, I cannot ignore it. I can't turn it off. . . . As I reach out to turn off the set, the strength goes out of my arms. So I sit there for hours and hours." An immature youth? No, this was a college English instructor! But youths too can be TV junkies. Note the reactions of some who agreed to a "No TV Week":

"I've been having a state of depression . . . I'm going out of my mind."—Twelve-year-old Susan.

"I don't think I'll be able to kick the habit. I love TV too much."—Thirteen-year-old Linda.

"The pressure was on terribly. I kept on having the urge. The hardest time was nighttime between eight and ten o'clock."—Eleven-year-old Louis.

It is no surprise, then, that most of the youths involved celebrated the end of "No TV Week" with a mad dash for the TV set. But far from being something to laugh at, TV addiction brings with it a host of potential problems. Consider just a few of them:

Slipping grades: The National Institute of Mental

Health (U.S.) reported that excessive TV viewing can lead to "lower school achievement, especially in reading." The book *The Literacy Hoax* further charges: "Television's effect on children is to create an expectation that learning should be easy, passive, and entertaining." The TV addict may thus find studying an ordeal.

Poor reading habits: When was the last time you picked up a book and read it from cover to cover? A spokesman for the West German Association of Book Dealers lamented: "We have become a nation of people who go home after work and fall asleep in front of the television. We are reading less and less." A report from Australia similarly said: "For every hour spent reading, the average Australian child will have seen seven hours of television."

Diminished family life: Wrote one Christian woman: "Because of excessive TV viewing . . . I was very lonely and felt isolated. It was as if [my] family were all strangers." Do you likewise find yourself spending less time with your family because of TV?

Laziness: Some feel that the very passiveness of TV "may lead to [a youth's] expectation that [his] needs will be met without effort and to a passive approach to life."

Exposure to unwholesome influences: Some cable television networks bring pornography into the home. And regular programming often provides a steady diet of car crashes, explosions, stabbings, shootings, and karate kicks. According to one estimate, a young person in the United States will witness the killing of 18,000 people on TV by the time he is 14 years old, not to mention fistfights and vandalism.

YOUNG PEOPLE ASK . . .

TV viewing is a serious addiction for some

British researcher William Belson found that boys who thrived on violent TV shows were more likely to "engage in violence of a serious kind." He also claimed that TV violence could incite "swearing and the use of bad language, aggressiveness in sport or play, threatening to use violence on another boy, writing slogans on walls, [and] breaking windows." While you may think yourself immune to such influences, Belson's study found that exposure to TV violence did not "change [the] boys' *conscious attitudes* toward" violence. The steady diet of violence apparently chipped away at their *subconscious* inhibitions against violence.

Of even more concern, though, is the effect addiction to TV violence can have upon one's relationship with the God who 'hates anyone loving violence.' —Psalm 11:5.

How Can I Control My Viewing?

This does not necessarily mean that TV must be viewed as inherently evil. Writer Vance Packard points out: "Much that is on U.S. television can be rewarding . . . Often there are early evening programs that are magnificent achievements in photography showing nature at work—from the activities of bats, beavers, bison to those of blowfish. Public television has stunning

'I Was a TV Addict'—An Interview

Interviewer: How old were you when you got hooked on TV?

Wyant: About ten years old. As soon as I came home from school, I'd turn on the TV. First, I'd watch the cartoons and kiddie programs. Then the news would come on, . . . and I'd go into the kitchen and look for something to eat. After that, I'd go back to the TV and watch till I wanted to go to sleep.

Interviewer: But when did you have time for your friends?

Wyant: The TV was my friend.

Interviewer: Then you never had time for play or sports?

Wyant: [laughing] I have no athletic abilities. Because I watched TV all the time, I never developed them. I'm a terrible basketball player. And in gym class I was always the last one to get chosen. I wish, though, I had developed my athletic abilities a bit more—not so that I could have gone around boasting, but just so I could have at least enjoyed myself.

Interviewer: What about your grades?

Wyant: I managed in grammar school. I'd stay up late and do my homework at the last minute. But it was harder in high school because I had developed such poor study habits.

Interviewer: Has watching all that TV affected you?

Wyant: Yes. Sometimes when I'm around people, I find myself

ballet, opera, and chamber music. TV is very good at covering important events . . . Occasionally TV comes up with illuminating dramatic productions."

Nevertheless, even too much of a *good* thing can be harmful. (Compare Proverbs 25:27.) And if you find you lack the self-control to turn off harmful shows, it is good to remember the words of the apostle Paul: "I am not going to let anything make me its slave." (1 Corin-

just watching them—as if I were watching a TV talk show—instead of participating in the conversation. I wish I could relate better to people.

Interviewer: *Well, you've done just fine in this conversation. Obviously you've overcome your addiction.*

Wyant: *I started breaking away from TV after I entered high school. . . . I sought out the association of Witness youths and started to make spiritual progress.*

Interviewer: *But what did this have to do with your TV viewing?*

Wyant: *As my appreciation for spiritual things grew, I realized that many of the shows I used to watch really weren't for Christians. Too, I felt the need to do more study of the Bible and to prepare for Christian meetings. That meant cutting out most of the TV viewing. It wasn't easy, though. I used to love those Saturday-morning cartoons. But then a Christian brother in the congregation invited me to go with him in the door-to-door preaching work on Saturday morning. That broke my Saturday morning TV habit. So eventually I learned really to tone down my TV watching.*

Interviewer: *What about today?*

Wyant: *Well, I still have the problem that if the TV is on, I cannot get anything done. So I leave it off most of the time. In fact, my TV broke down a few months ago and I haven't bothered to get it fixed.*

thians 6:12, *Today's English Version*) How, then, can you break free from slavery to TV and control your viewing?

Writer Linda Nielsen observes: "Self-control begins by learning to set goals." First, analyze your present habits. For a week, keep track of what shows you watch and how much time you spend each day in front of the tube. Do you turn it on the very minute you get home?

When do you turn it off? How many shows are "must-sees" every week? You might be shocked by the results.

Then take a hard look at what shows you've been watching. "Does not the ear itself test out words as the palate tastes food?" asks the Bible. (Job 12:11) So use discernment (along with the advice of your parents) and test out what shows are really worth seeing. Some determine in advance what shows they will watch and turn on the TV *only for those shows!* Others take sterner measures, establishing no-television-during-the-school-week rules or one-hour-a-day limits.

But what if a silent TV set proves just too much of a temptation? One family solved the problem this way: "We keep our set in the basement to have it out of the way . . . In the basement there's less of a temptation to just flick it on when you enter the house. You have to make a special trip down there to watch something." Keeping your set in the closet, or merely leaving it unplugged, may work just as effectively.

Interestingly, amid all their 'withdrawal pangs' the youths participating in "No TV Week" found some positive substitutes for TV. One girl recalled: "I talked to my mom. She became a much more interesting person in

When a television is placed in an inconvenient location, there is less temptation to turn it on

my view, because my attentions were not divided between her and the television set." Another girl passed the time trying her hand at cooking. A young boy named Jason even discovered it could be fun to go "to the park instead of TV," or to fish, read, or go to the beach.

> "*I*'ve been having a state of depression . . . I'm going out of my mind."—Twelve-year-old Susan, a participant in "No TV Week"

The experience of Wyant (see insert entitled "I Was a TV Addict") illustrates that another key to controlling TV viewing is having "plenty to do in the work of the Lord." (1 Corinthians 15: 58) You too will find that drawing close to God, studying the Bible with the help of the many fine publications now available, and busying yourself in God's work will help you overcome an addiction to TV. (James 4:8) True, limiting your TV viewing will mean missing some of your favorite programs. But why must you use TV to the full, slavishly following every single program? (See 1 Corinthians 7:29, 31.) Better it is to 'get tough' with yourself like the apostle Paul, who once said: "I pummel my body and lead it as a slave." (1 Corinthians 9:27) Isn't this better than being a slave of a TV set?

Questions for Discussion   *Chapter 36*

☐ *Why can TV viewing be called an addiction for some youths?*

☐ *What are some potentially damaging effects of excessive TV viewing?*

☐ *What are some ways of controlling TV viewing?*

☐ *What can you do in place of watching TV?*

Chapter 37

Why Can't I
Have a Good Time
Once in a While?

ON Friday evenings, Pauline* used to go to Christian meetings. She enjoyed the discussions, but she would sometimes resent the fact that she was there and her school friends were out having a good time.

When the meeting was over, Pauline would pass by a local teen hangout on her way home. She recalls: "Attracted by the loud music and flashing lights, I would press my nose to the window as we passed and longingly imagine the fun they must be having." In time, her desire to enjoy herself with her friends became the most important thing in her life.

Like Pauline, you may sometimes feel that because you are a Christian, you are missing out on something. You want to watch that TV show all the others are talking about, but your parents say it is too violent. You want to go to the mall and hang out with the kids at school, but your parents call them "bad associations." (1 Corinthians 15:33) You want to go to that party all your schoolmates will attend, but Mom and Dad say no.

Your schoolmates seem to come and go as they please, attending concerts and partying till the break of dawn without the interference of their parents. You may

* Not her real name.

YOUNG PEOPLE ASK . . .

thus find yourself envying their freedom. Not that you want to do anything bad. You just want to have a good time once in a while.

Recreation—God's View

Be assured that there is nothing wrong with wanting to enjoy yourself. After all, Jehovah is "the happy God." (1 Timothy 1:11) And through the wise man Solomon, He says: "Young people, enjoy your youth. Be happy while you are still young. Do what you want to do, and follow your heart's desire." However, Solomon then warned: "Remember that God is going to judge you for whatever you do."—Ecclesiastes 11:9, 10, *Today's English Version.*

> "**A**ttracted by the loud music and flashing lights, I would press my nose to the window as we passed and longingly imagine the fun they must be having"

Knowing that God holds you responsible for your actions puts recreation in an entirely different light. For while God does not condemn one for having a good time, he does disapprove of one who is a 'lover of pleasure,' a person who lives only for the next good time. (2 Timothy 3:1, 4) Why is this? Consider King Solomon. Using his vast resources, he tasted of every conceivable human pleasure. He says: "Anything that my eyes asked for I did not keep away from them. I did not hold back my heart from any sort of rejoicing." The outcome? "Look! everything was vanity and a striving after wind." (Ecclesiastes 2:10, 11) Yes, God knows that in the long run, a life of pleasure-seeking only leaves you empty and frustrated.

God also requires that you stay free of defiling practices, such as drug abuse and premarital sex. (2 Corinthians 7:1) Yet, many of the things teenagers do for fun can lead to one's being ensnared in these practices. One young girl, for example, decided to attend an unchaperoned gathering of some schoolmates. "The music on the stereo was terrific, great dancing, neat refreshments and plenty of laughs," she recalls. But then, "someone brought pot. Then came the booze. That's when everything started to go haywire." Sexual immorality resulted. Confessed the girl: "I have been miserable and depressed ever since." Without adult supervision, how easily such gatherings become "wild parties," or revelries!—Galatians 5:21, *Byington.*

No wonder that your parents may be very concerned about how you spend your leisure time, perhaps restricting where you can go and whom you can associate with. Their motive? To help you heed God's warning: "Remove vexation from your heart, and ward off calamity from your flesh; for youth and the prime of life are vanity."—Ecclesiastes 11:10.

Envious of Pleasure-Seekers?

It is easy to forget all of this and envy the freedom some youths seem to enjoy. Pauline stopped attending Christian meetings and got in with a pleasure-seeking crowd. "I found myself practicing all the wrong things I had been warned against," she recalls. Pauline's pleasure binge eventually resulted in her arrest and placement in a school for wayward girls!

Long ago the writer of Psalm 73 had feelings similar to Pauline's. "I became envious of the boasters, when I would see the very peace of wicked people," he confessed. He even began to doubt the value of living by righteous principles. "Surely it is in vain that I have cleansed my heart and that I wash my hands in innocence itself," he said. But then a profound insight came to him: Wicked people are "on slippery ground," teetering on the brink of disaster!—Psalm 73:3, 13, 18.

Do youths who follow Bible principles really miss out on a good time?

Pauline learned this—the hard way. After her worldly fling, she made drastic changes in her life in order to regain God's favor. You, on the other hand, do not have to suffer arrest, contract a sexually transmitted disease, or go through the agonies of drug withdrawal to realize that the cost of a 'good time' can be far too high. There are many wholesome, upbuilding ways to enjoy oneself that are free of such risks. What are some of them?

Wholesome Good Times

A survey of American youths revealed that teenagers "enjoy occasional family outings and activities." Doing things together as a family not only is fun but can enhance family unity.

This means more than simply watching TV together. Says Dr. Anthony Pietropinto: "The problem with television-viewing is that, while it may be done in the company of others, it is basically a solitary activity. . . . Yet, pastimes such as indoor games, backyard sports, cooking treats, crafts projects, and reading aloud certainly offer greater opportunities for communication, cooperation, and intellectual stimulation than does the modern family's passive preoccupation with television." As John, a father of seven, says: 'Even cleaning the yard or painting the house can be fun when it is done as a family.'

Taking up a hobby is one wholesome way of using free time

If your family is not already doing such things together, take the initiative and suggest them to your parents. Try coming up with some interesting and exciting ideas for family outings or projects.

You do not always have to be with others, however, to enjoy yourself. Mary, a youth who carefully watches her associations, has learned how to enjoy her times alone. "I play the piano and the violin, and I spend some time practicing them," she says. Melissa, another teenage girl, similarly says: "I sometimes spend time writing stories or poetry for my own enjoyment." You too can learn to use time productively by developing skills such as reading, carpentry, or playing a musical instrument.

Christian Gatherings

From time to time, it is also enjoyable to get together with friends. And in many areas there are any number of wholesome activities you can enjoy. Bowling, skating, bicycle riding, baseball, and basketball are popular activities in North America. You might also branch out and try visiting a museum or a zoo. And, yes, there is a place for

YOUNG PEOPLE ASK . . .

getting together and simply playing records or watching a wholesome TV show with fellow Christian youths.

You might even ask your parents to help you plan a more formal gathering. Make it interesting by arranging for a variety of activities, such as party games and group singing. If some of your friends have musical talents, perhaps they can be coaxed into performing a bit. Good food also adds to an occasion, but it does not have to be fancy or expensive. Sometimes guests can bring different food items.

Is there a park or an outdoor area nearby that allows for activities such as playing ball or swimming? Why not plan a picnic? Again, families can share in bringing food so that no one is burdened financially.

Moderation is the key. Music does not need to be at ear-splitting levels to be enjoyed, nor does dancing have to be vulgar or sensual to be fun. Similarly, outdoor

Christian gatherings are more enjoyable when various activities are planned and different age-groups are represented

games can be enjoyed without cutthroat competition. Yet, reports one parent: "Some youths at times argue, almost to the point of fighting." Keep such activities enjoyable by following the Bible's advice to avoid 'competing with one another.'—Galatians 5:26.

"Someone brought pot. Then came the booze. That's when everything started to go haywire"

Whom should you invite? The Bible says, "Have love for the whole association of brothers." (1 Peter 2:17) Why limit your gatherings to peers? Widen out in your associations. (Compare 2 Corinthians 6:13.) One parent observed: "The elderly, though often not able to participate in some of the activities, enjoy coming and watching the goings-on." The presence of adults often helps prevent things from getting out of hand. It is not possible, though, to invite "the whole association" to any one gathering. Besides, smaller gatherings are easier to control.

Christian gatherings also present the opportunity to build one another up spiritually. True, some youths feel that adding spirituality to a gathering takes the fun out of it. "When we have a gathering," complained one Christian boy, "it's, 'Sit down, get your Bible out, and play Bible games.'" However, the psalmist said: "Happy is the man . . . [whose] delight is in the law of Jehovah." (Psalm 1:1, 2) Discussions—or even games—that center around the Bible can thus be quite enjoyable. Perhaps you simply need to sharpen your knowledge of the Scriptures so as to be able to participate more fully.

Another idea is to have several relate how they became Christians. Or add a dose of warmth and laughter by inviting some to tell humorous stories. Often these teach valuable lessons. Some of the chapters in this book may even form the basis for an interesting group discussion at a gathering.

Keep Recreation in Balance!

Jesus Christ was certainly not above having a good time once in a while. The Bible tells of his attending a wedding feast in Cana, where food, music, dancing, and upbuilding association no doubt abounded. Jesus even made a contribution to the success of the wedding feast by miraculously providing wine!—John 2:3-11.

But Jesus' life was not a nonstop party. He spent most of his time pursuing spiritual interests, teaching people the will of God. Said he: "My food is for me to do the will of him that sent me and to finish his work." (John 4:34) Doing God's will brought Jesus far more lasting pleasure than some temporary diversion would have. Today, there is still "plenty to do in the work of the Lord." (1 Corinthians 15:58; Matthew 24:14) But when, from time to time, you feel the need for some recreation, enjoy it in a balanced, wholesome way. As one writer put it: "Life can't always be jam-packed full of action and excitement—and you'd probably be exhausted if it were!"

Questions for Discussion	*Chapter 37*

☐ *Why do some Christian youths envy youths of the world? Have you ever felt that way?*

☐ *What caution does God give youths regarding their conduct, and how should this affect their choice of recreation?*

☐ *Why is it foolish to envy youths who violate God's laws and principles?*

☐ *What are some ways to enjoy wholesome recreation (1) with family members, (2) by yourself, and (3) with fellow Christians?*

☐ *How did Jesus Christ set an example in balance when it comes to recreation?*

Your Future

Today's youths have grown up under the threat of having no future at all. Nuclear war, ecological disaster, and economic chaos all loom large on the horizon. The fate of mankind, however, may be the least of your worries. You may be far more concerned with where you will be 10, 20, or 30 years from now.

Fortunately, there is real reason for you to be optimistic about your future. This depends upon how you utilize the present.

Chapter 38

What Does the Future Hold for Me?

"I AM afraid of the future, a future in a world character-ized by nuclear threats." Thus spoke a German youth in an address to his nation's highest political official.

Perhaps the specter of perishing in a nuclear fireball likewise haunts your vision of the future. "Why should I bother to get good grades?" asked one youth. "The world's going to blow up anyway." Indeed, in one survey of schoolchildren, young boys cited nuclear war as their greatest fear. Girls rated it second, preceded only by the fear of "my parents' dying."

A nuclear mushroom, however, is not the only dark cloud on the horizon. The threat of "overpopulation, exhaustion of resources, pollution of the environment," and other impending disasters led famed psychologist B. F. Skinner to conclude: "Our species now appears to be threatened." He later confessed: "I'm very pessimis-tic. We're not going to solve our problems, really."

Since even learned observers view the future with trepidation, it is little wonder that many youths display the attitude: "Let us eat and drink, for tomorrow we are to die." (1 Corinthians 15:32) Indeed, if your future rides on the ability of politicians and scientists, it looks grim, indeed. For Jeremiah 10:23 says: "To earthling man his way does not belong. It does not belong to man who is walking even to direct his step."

It is not that man simply lacks the ability to govern

himself. Note that it does not "belong" to man to do so —he has no right to manage earth's future. His efforts are thus doomed to failure. For that reason, Jeremiah prayed for divine intervention: "Correct me, O Jehovah, however with judgment." (Jeremiah 10:24) This means that our Creator will determine our future. But what will that future be?

God's Purpose for Earth—And Your Future

Shortly after man's creation, God told the first human couple: "Be fruitful and become many and fill the earth and subdue it, and have in subjection the fish of the sea and the flying creatures of the heavens and every living creature that is moving upon the earth." (Genesis 1:28) Man was thus presented with the prospect of living in a global paradise.

> "I'm very pessimistic. We're not going to solve our problems, really."
> —Psychologist B. F. Skinner

The first couple, however, rebelled at God's rulership. As Solomon later put it, "The true God made mankind upright, but they themselves have sought out many plans." (Ecclesiastes 7:29) Human plans have proved to be disastrous, leaving the present generation a legacy of misery and the most dismal of future prospects.

Does this mean that God has abandoned the earth to becoming a polluted, radioactive—and perhaps lifeless—globe? Impossible! He is "the Former of the earth and the Maker of it, He the One who firmly established it, who did not create it simply for nothing, who formed it even to be inhabited." His stated purpose for the earth is thus sure to be fulfilled!—Isaiah 45:18; 55:10, 11.

But when—and how? Read for yourself Luke chap-

Earth's Creator will not allow man to ruin our planet

ter 21. There Jesus predicted the very problems that have plagued mankind during this century: international wars, earthquakes, disease, food shortages, widespread crime. What do these events signify? Jesus himself explains: "As these things start to occur, raise yourselves erect and lift your heads up, because your deliverance is getting near. . . . When you see these things occurring, know that the kingdom of God is near."—Luke 21:10, 11, 28, 31.

That Kingdom is the key to your future. Simply stated, it is a government, God's means of ruling earth. That Kingdom government will forcibly wrest control of earth from human hands. (Daniel 2:44) "Those ruining the earth" will themselves face ruin at God's hands, saving the earth—and mankind—from the onslaughts of human abuse.—Revelation 11:18; Ecclesiastes 1:4.

Secure under the management of God's Kingdom, the earth will gradually become a global paradise. (Luke 23:43) A perfect ecological balance will thus return. Why, there will even be harmony between man and beast. (Isaiah 11:6-9) War and weapons of war will disappear. (Psalm 46:8, 9) Crime, hunger, housing shortages, sickness—even death itself—will all be eliminated. Earth's inhabitants "will indeed find their exquisite delight in the abundance of peace."—Psalm 37:10, 11; 72:16; Isaiah 65:21, 22; Revelation 21:3, 4.

'Testing' God's Promises

Everlasting life in a paradise—that can be *your* future! But while the idea may sound appealing, perhaps you have difficulty letting go of the belief that all good people go to heaven, or you have doubts about the Bible itself. Even some youths among Jehovah's Witnesses have found their faith at times to be alarmingly wobbly. Michelle, for example, was raised by Witness parents. Accepting that the Bible is true was like accepting that day followed night. One day, though, it dawned on her—she didn't know *why* she believed the Bible. "I guess I believed it up till then because my mother and father believed it," she said.

"Without faith it is impossible to please [God] well," says the Bible. (Hebrews 11:6) Yet, faith is not something you possess because your mother and father have it. If your future is to be secure, you must build a faith based on solid evidence—an "assured expectation of things hoped for." (Hebrews 11:1) As the Bible puts it, you must "make sure of all things," or as the paraphrase in *The Living Bible* expresses it, "test everything that is said to be sure it is true."—1 Thessalonians 5:21.

Proving to Yourself That the Bible Is True

You may first need to test whether the Bible is truly "inspired of God." (2 Timothy 3:16) How can you do that? Well, only Almighty God can without fail 'tell from the beginning the finale.' (Isaiah 43:9; 46:10) And he does so repeatedly in the Bible. Read the prophecies recorded at Luke 19:41-44 and 21:20, 21 regarding the fall of Jerusalem. Or the prophecies at Isaiah 44:27, 28 and 45:1-4 regarding the fall of Babylon. Secular history proves how unerringly the Bible predicted these events! "After examining some of its prophecies," said 14-year-old Janine, "I was just amazed to see how it was able to foretell all that it did."

The Bible's historical accuracy, honesty, candor, and lack of contradiction are further reasons to put faith in the Bible.* But how do you know that the way Jehovah's Witnesses understand the Bible is correct? The inhabitants of ancient Beroea did not accept the apostle Paul's explanation of the Bible unquestioningly. Rather, they 'examined the Scriptures daily as to whether these things were so.'—Acts 17:11.

We urge you likewise to make an in-depth study of the Bible's teachings. The publications *You Can Live Forever in Paradise on Earth* and *United in Worship of the Only True God* (published by the Watchtower Bible and Tract Society of New York, Inc.) set forth these

---

* See pages 58-68 of the publication *Reasoning From the Scriptures* (published by the Watchtower Bible and Tract Society of New York, Inc.) for more detailed information regarding the authenticity of the Bible.

Have you convinced yourself of the truthfulness of the Bible?

teachings in a clear manner. If your parents are Jehovah's Witnesses, they will no doubt be able to help you with any questions you might have. "Be honest with your parents if you have any problems in this regard," suggests a young woman named Janel. "Ask questions if there is something you find difficult to believe." (Proverbs 15:22) In time you will no doubt come to appreciate that Jehovah has indeed blessed his Witnesses with a marvelous understanding of Bible truths!

Says a youth named Prentice: "Sometimes I get depressed over how the world is. I look up scriptures such as Revelation 21:4, and it gives me something to hope for." Yes, having solid faith in God's promises is sure to affect your outlook. You view the future with happy anticipation, not gloom. Your present life becomes, not an aimless struggle, but a means of 'safely treasuring up for yourself a fine foundation for the future, in order that you may get a firm hold on the real life.'—1 Timothy 6:19.

But is there more to attaining that "real life" than simply learning and coming to believe the Bible's teachings?

Questions for Discussion   Chapter 38

☐ *What fears do many youths have regarding their future?*

☐ *What was God's original purpose for the earth? Why can we be confident that God's purpose has not changed?*

☐ *What role does the Kingdom play in fulfilling God's purpose for the earth?*

☐ *Why is it necessary that you test the truthfulness of the Bible's teachings, and how can you do so?*

☐ *How can you prove to yourself that the Bible is inspired by God?*

Chapter 39

How Can I Get Close to God?

CLOSE—to God? To many people, God seems to be an aloof, distant figure, an impersonal 'First Cause.' The idea of being close to him may thus seem disquieting, even frightening to you.

Then again, your experience may be like that of a young woman named Lynda. Lynda was raised by Christian parents and recalls: "In all [my teen] years, I rarely missed a Christian meeting, and I have never missed a month of preaching activity, yet I never really developed a close personal relationship with Jehovah."

Is it really possible for me to be close to God?

Your very future, though, depends upon your getting close to God. Said Jesus Christ: "This means everlasting life, their taking in knowledge of you, the only true God." (John 17:3) This "knowledge" is more than the ability to learn or recite facts—an atheist could do that. It involves cultivating a relationship with God, becoming his friend. (Compare James 2:23.) Far from being unapproachable, God invites us to "seek . . . and really find him," for "he is not far off from each one of us."—Acts 17:27.

How You Can Come to Know God

Have you ever gazed at the distant stars, listened with wonderment to the roaring sea, been enchanted by a graceful butterfly, or marveled at the delicate beauty of a tiny leaf? These works of God all give but a glimpse of his immense power, wisdom, and love. God's "invisible qualities . . . are perceived by the things made, even his eternal power and Godship."—Romans 1:19, 20.

The Bible is God's revelation to man. It tells us how we got here and where we are going

However, you need to know more about God than creation alone can reveal. God has therefore provided his written Word. That book reveals God to be, not some nameless entity or impersonal force, but a real Person with a name. "Know that Jehovah is God," declares the psalmist. (Psalm 100:3) The Bible also reveals the Person behind that name: "a God merciful and gracious, slow to anger and abundant in loving-kindness and truth." (Exodus 34:6) Its detailed record of God's dealings with mankind allows us, in effect, to see God in action! Reading the Bible is thus an essential part of getting close to God.

Making Bible Reading Pleasurable

Admittedly, the Bible is a long book to read. Its sheer bulk often frightens youths away from reading it. Some also complain that the Bible is boring. The Bible, though, is God's revelation to man. It tells us how we got here and where we are going. It spells out exactly what we must do to live forever in Paradise on earth. How could that possibly be boring? Granted, the Bible is not light reading, and in it are "some things hard to understand." (2 Peter 3:16) But Bible reading need not be drudgery.

...the pit of death and ...the hole. And in the enshroud-...furry presence rubs up against you . . .

Boring? Hardly! But remember: You are not reading to be entertained. Try to discern what the account teaches about Jehovah. For example, do not Daniel's experiences demonstrate that Jehovah allows his servants to face difficult trials?

Try, also, to have a regular reading schedule. Why, if you spend just 15 minutes a day reading the Bible, you might be able to complete it in about a year! 'Buy out the time' from some less important activity—like TV watching. (Ephesians 5:16) As you apply yourself to Bible reading, you are bound to feel closer than ever to God.—Proverbs 2:1, 5.

Prayer Draws You Close to Him

A teenage girl named Laverne observed, "It's hard to really have a personal relationship with someone you don't talk to him." As the "Hearer of prayer," Jehovah invites us to talk to him. (Psalm 65:2) If we approach him in faith, "no matter what it is that we ask according to his will, he hears us."—1 John 5:14.

passively, try to imagine that you are Daniel. You have
been arrested on the outrageous charge of praying to
your God. The penalty? Death! Persian soldiers roughly
drag you to your tomb—a pit filled with hungry lions.
With a low rumble, the huge stone covering the pit is
rolled back. The lions below let loose spine-tingling
roars. Recoiling in horror, you are overpowered by the
king's soldiers, who pitch you into that pit. . . .
ing gloom, a faint . . . over tha . . .

CH. . .
you be te. . .
will also make . . . you
"in the lurch." (1 Corin. . . 4:9)
Would you not feel closer to . . . . . .enced
his help in coping with a trial?

But do not pray only about personal problems. In his
model prayer, Jesus gave primary importance to the
sanctification of Jehovah's name, the coming of His
Kingdom, and the realization of God's will. (Matthew
9-13) "Supplication along with thanksgiving" is also
vital ingredient in prayer.—Philippians 4:6.

What if you simply find prayer awkward? Pray about that! Ask God to help you open your heart before him. "Persevere in prayer," and in time you will find that you can talk as freely to Jehovah as you do with a close friend. (Romans 12:12) "I know that whenever I have a problem," says young Maria, "I can turn to Jehovah for guidance and he will help me."

It is not necessary to address God with fancy or pretentious language. "Before him pour out your heart," said the psalmist. (Psalm 62:8) Let him know your feelings, your concerns. Ask him for help in dealing with your weaknesses. Pray for his blessing upon your family and upon fellow Christians. Beg him for forgiveness when you err. Thank him daily for the gift of life. When prayer becomes a regular part of your life, it can bring you into a close and happy relationship with Jehovah God.

Publicly Declaring Your Friendship With God

Having begun to enjoy a friendship with God, should you not be eager to help others gain that precious relationship too? Indeed, it is a requirement for those who wish to be God's friends that they make "public declaration for salvation."—Romans 10:10.

Many begin by sharing their faith informally, talking

*R*eading the Bible is essential to developing friendship with God

Meetings—An Aid in Getting Close to God

"**I have found** that close association with others who love Jehovah helps me to stay close to him." So said one young Nigerian youth. Jehovah's Witnesses arrange for such periods of association at their local Kingdom Halls. (Hebrews 10:23-25) Said 16-year-old Anita: "In the Kingdom Hall, I found real friends."

However, such gatherings are not mere social functions. Kingdom Halls offer a course of Bible education, consisting of five weekly meetings. A wide range of topics is covered: family life, Bible prophecy, conduct, doctrine, and the Christian ministry, to name a few. Though not elaborate stage productions, such meetings are presented in an interesting way. Talks and group discussions are often interspersed with interviews and lively sketches. The Theocratic Ministry School is particularly outstanding in that it has trained thousands to be effective public speakers.

What if you are already attending meetings? Strive to get more out of them. (1) <u>Prepare</u>: "I've set aside fixed times to study the books we use at the meetings," says Anita. This will make it easier for you to (2) <u>Participate</u>: As a youth, Jesus actively listened, asked questions, and gave answers when spiritual matters were discussed in the temple.

to schoolmates, neighbors, and relatives. Later on, they join Jehovah's Witnesses in their work of preaching "from house to house." (Acts 5:42) For some youths, though, this public work is a stumbling block. "I think a lot of young people are embarrassed to go from house to house," says one young Christian. "They're afraid of how their friends will look at them."

But whose approval do you really value—that of your peers or that of your heavenly Friend, Jehovah? Should you let fear or embarrassment hinder you from

(Luke 2:46, 47) You too can "pay more than the usual attention to the things heard," taking notes to keep your mind on track. (Hebrews 2:1) When audience participation is called for, have a share in commenting.

Another helpful suggestion is to (3) Use what you learn: Share points you learn with others. More important, apply what you learn to your life, making changes where needed. Show that the truth is "at work in you."—1 Thessalonians 2:13.

Give meetings priority. If you have an exceptionally heavy load of homework, try doing it before the meeting.

"I love to chat after meetings and stay till the last," says a youth named Simeon. "But when I have schoolwork, I leave right away to do my work." However you work matters out, do what you can to be at meetings regularly. They are vital to your spiritual growth.

gaining salvation? "Let us hold fast the public declaration of our hope without wavering," urges the apostle Paul. (Hebrews 10:23) And you will find that with sufficient training and preparation, you can begin to find real joy in the preaching work!—1 Peter 3:15.

In due time your appreciation for your heavenly Friend should move you to make an unreserved dedication to God and to symbolize it by water baptism. (Romans 12:1; Matthew 28:19, 20) Making a public declaration to become a baptized disciple of Christ is

"I know that whenever I have a problem I can turn to Jehovah for guidance and he will help me"

not something to be taken lightly. It involves 'disowning yourself'—setting aside personal ambitions and seeking first the interests of Jehovah God. (Mark 8:34) It further involves identifying yourself with the worldwide organization of Jehovah's Witnesses.

"I think a lot of young people hesitate to get baptized," observed a youth named Robert. "They fear it's a final step that they can't back out of." True, one cannot back out of a dedication to God. (Compare Ecclesiastes 5:4.) But "if one knows how to do what is right and yet does not do it, it is a sin for him"—baptized or unbaptized! (James 4:17) The issue is, Do you appreciate God's friendship? Are you moved to want to serve him forever? Then do not let fear hinder you from proclaiming yourself a friend of God!

Eternal Benefits for God's Friends!

Choosing God's friendship will put you at odds with the whole world. (John 15:19) You may become the target of ridicule. Difficulties, problems, and temptations may assail you. But do not let anyone or anything rob you of your relationship with God. He promises his

YOUNG PEOPLE ASK . . .